RZ

X 54

GW01459096

RZ

A GREEK
EXPERIENCE
1943–1948

EPIRUS

0   5   10 Miles

0   5   10 15 20 Kilometres

MACEDONIA

Mount Grammos

Nemersika Mountains

ALBANIA

Leskovits

Pendalophos

Sarandoporos R.

Smolikas Mountains

Pindas Mountains

Argyrokastro

Mount Merope

Melissopetra

Konitsa

Aoos R.

Vasiliko

Konitsa Plain

Mount Gamcela

Papingo

Timfi Mountains

Delvinaki

Vikos Gorge

Tsepelovo

Doliana

Monodendri

Aoos R.

Kalpaki

Vitsi

Zygos Pass

Kalamas R.

Mitsikeli Mountains

Metsovo

Mount Morgana

Zitsa

Perama

Lake of Ioannina

IOANNINA

Kastritza

Filiates

Dodona

Pramanda

Menina

Mt.Olytsika

Plaisia

Igoumenitsa

LAKKASOULI

Tseritsana

Varyiadhes

Agnanda

Paramythia

Plaka

Tzoumerka Mountains

Souli Mountains

Derviziana

Xerovouni Mountains

Acheron R.

Arakhthos R.

IONIAN SEA

Parga

Threspotiko

Philippeas

Louros

Arta

YUGOSLAVIA

Durazzo

Bitolj (Monastir)

Lake Okhrid

(Pelagonia)

ALBANIA

Edessa

Salonika

Valona

MACEDONIA

Trikala

Larisa

THESSALY

Ioannina

Volos

CORFU

EPIRUS

Paxoi

Arta

Preveza

LEVKAS

ACARNANIA

IONIAN SEA

Ithaka

AETOLIA

CEPHALONIA

Patras

Athens

Corinth

0   50 Miles

Louros R.

Preveza

Mt. Acteion

Amphilokia

A GREEK EXPERIENCE

1943–1948

NIGEL CLIVE

WITH AN INTRODUCTION BY

SIR WILLIAM DEAKIN

MICHAEL RUSSELL

For Maria
who was my reward
at the end of it all

© Nigel Clive 1985

First published in Great Britain 1985
by Michael Russell (Publishing) Ltd
The Chantry, Wilton, Salisbury, Wiltshire

Typeset in Linotron Sabon
at The Spartan Press Limited, Lymington, Hampshire
Printed and bound in Great Britain
by Biddles Ltd, Guildford and King's Lynn

ISBN 0 85955 119 9

Contents

Acknowledgements

I am especially grateful to Sir William Deakin for his initial suggestion that I should record my wartime experience of the Resistance in mountain Greece in 1944, and for much subsequent assistance. I have also greatly benefited from discussing various aspects of this text with the Hon. C. M. Woodhouse, Mr Nicholas Rizopoulos and Mr Lars Baerentzen, to each of whom I express my deep gratitude. In addition, I wish to thank Ms Linda Wrigley for her editorial advice and Ms Carol Rath for typing the final version with such speed and accuracy. To my wife I owe very much more than the customary expression of thanks for her constant help and encouragement at every turn.

Introduction

This book tells the story of a British military mission parachuted to northern Greece in December 1943. It is by no means a mere addition to a list of such events.

It has its own fresh and vivid contribution to make, and, against a neat background in which the author sketches the confused setting of Greek politics at the time, he conveys the daily work and trials of operating such a party in the lonely and barren regions of Epirus. He became a natural expert on its political geography, and brushes keen and sympathetic portraits of his brother officers and wireless operators with other roving missions, and, above all, of his Greek agents, their families, and the perilous structure of their activities.

The task of Nigel Clive was precise: to report in detail on the German order of battle throughout the area. This implied the careful building up of a network of local informers to penetrate the German-held towns and bases, and to establish cautious cooperation with Greek partisan units in ambushing German patrols and isolated garrisons, thus gathering identity papers, regimental numbers and other essential details.

This book is of particular historical interest, as the story of this mission is set against the account, written in later captivity, of the German military commander in northern Greece, Lieutenant General Hubert Lanz of the XXII Mountain Corps. This German picture of the region as a setting for guerrilla warfare is written with perception in both geographical and psychological terms. Lanz's account of the countryside, the constant menace by the enemy to the road and rail communications of the area of his command is of rare value. As he wrote: 'Constantly watched by the partisans and their numerous accomplices in the city and reported in advance to the bands in the countryside, the German columns moved in guarded convoys . . . During the entire period of the occupation, hardly a night, and from the summer of 1944, not a single day passed without a surprise attack, a mine explosion or another act of sabotage on one of the supply roads . . . A stranger became lost in this stony desert.' The events described in this book are, in the main, confined to Epirus and territory where the EDES bands of General Zervas were stationed. The portrait of Zervas is a model: 'His vast bulk seemed to envelop the small working desk in front of him where the papers were hidden by his Old Testament beard. With a forage cap worn jauntily on one side of his huge head and a sparkle in his eyes, he was the picture-book guerrilla . . . I had been expecting something different, someone less self-assured.'

It is beyond the range of this brief introduction to comment on the intricacies of inter-Greek clashes, but to commend the effective work of an intelligence mission, which is described in this book, working in isolation, and at daily risk.

The British authorities in Cairo were receiving a mass of evidence on the German order of battle and further political reports on EDES territory, some of which appear for the first time in this account. These latter documents still no controversies, such as Zervas's contacts with the Germans, but enrich the evidence. The final withdrawal of the German forces under Lanz from Greece and its local repercussions, is a piece of high local drama.

Nigel Clive was a witness of the confused beginning of the sombre events in Athens in December 1944, which he describes in detail, but he was ordered to report to London before the arrival of Churchill and Eden on Christmas Day. He was to return to Athens as a member of the staff of the British Embassy until 1948. His first experience of Greece had been during the campaign of 1941 as an officer in the Middlesex Yeomanry. In 1949 he married a charming Greek wife. The country and its people remain a central part of his life. This record of the formative years – an accident of irregular war – makes compelling reading.

F. W. DEAKIN

One

Everyone who was put ashore after 1940 or dropped by parachute in German-occupied Europe had volunteered for the job. No one was dragooned into any branch of the special forces which operated behind the German lines. Each one of us had, therefore, individual reasons for deciding to opt out of what he was doing before. In my case it was an urge that grew stronger through the summer of 1943 to leave the British Embassy in Baghdad where I was temporarily employed, and get back into the fighting war of which I had seen so little since it began. My only means of doing so was to apply for a special assignment, as the regiment I had joined as a Territorial officer before the war had been disbanded in 1941. Most people's lives are shaped by a mixture of certain events over which they had no control and others where personal decisions, sometimes resulting from chance encounters, have mapped the course ahead.

The circuitous route that brought me to Baghdad began at one such chance encounter during my last term at Oxford in May 1939 with Pat Gibson, a friend from my first year, who was then working in London. Our conversation turned to the likelihood of war and I went as far as saying that it was inevitable. He then put me in my place by asking what steps I had taken to prepare for the inevitable. The answer was that I had done nothing whereas he, by contrast, had become an officer in the Territorial Army, which the Minister of War had doubled during that summer. By the end of lunch, I saw the logic of his decision and welcomed his encouragement to apply for a commission in the regiment he had joined, the 2nd Middlesex Yeomanry, which had been mechanized as Armoured Divisional Signals, as soon as I came down from Oxford. In June, to my surprise, the commanding officer accepted me.

At that time I held very strong views about the advances made by Nazi Germany and the pusillanimous attitude of the British government; but my interest in politics and especially in foreign affairs had taken longer to develop than in the case of many of my contemporaries. Coming from a family which had always voted Conservative, it was natural that when I went up to Christ Church, Oxford in 1936, I quickly joined the Carlton Club. As with so many of my generation, the event which first directed my attention to the international scene was the Spanish Civil War, when I found myself in instinctive opposition to Franco and progressively critical of Conservative foreign policy. A number of my friends shared this growing disillusionment with Neville Chamberlain and increasing respect for Churchill. Being no more of a misfit inside a Conservative club than they were, I was elected in the summer term of 1938 to serve as President from the start of the next academic year, beginning in the autumn. In my last long vacation in the summer of 1938, soon after my twenty-first birthday, I pooled my savings of £60 with one of my contemporaries, so that we could buy a Ford V8 two-seater in which we drove through Germany, Austria, Hungary, Yugoslavia and Albania with Greece as our destination. It was our first visit for both of us and we crammed into three hectic weeks of sightseeing glimpses of Delphi, Olympia, Mycenae, Epidaurus, Athens, Salonica and even Mount Athos. I was enchanted by the people and everything I saw. All the way there and back I felt in every sense closer to the Czech crisis and increasingly sure that we were on the road to war. When we returned shortly before Chamberlain signed away Czechoslovakia in the Munich agreement, my disgust was such that I determined to take action at the first opportunity. It was also the time that I began to keep a journal, much of which was devoted to recording my reactions to the procession of events leading to the war.

As soon as I returned to Oxford, I marched into the Carlton Club, turned Chamberlain's picture face to the wall and shortly thereafter announced my support for A. D. Lindsay, the Master of Balliol, who was standing in opposition to Quintin Hogg in the Oxford by-election, which was the first since Munich. I was warmly encouraged in my stand by three Christ Church dons – the economist Roy Harrod, Frank Pakenham (later the Earl of Longford) and Professor F. A. Lindemann, later Lord Cherwell, scientific adviser to Churchill during the Second World War. At my first meeting with Lindemann at the beginning of term in October 1938, he told me that in their last telephone conversation Churchill had called the Cabinet the Gadarene swine and had urged him to promote any form of political action by dissident Conservatives. Two weeks later Lindemann had drafted two parallel letters to the *Oxford Mail* and the *News Chronicle* explaining why Conservatives should vote against Hogg, which I had signed in the company of Teddy (as he was known in those days) Heath and Maurice Macmillan, the son of Harold Macmillan. When Quintin Hogg was elected at the end of October with a reduced majority, following a noisy demonstration by both town and gown where the slogan 'A vote for Hogg is a vote for Hitler' was shouted, I decided to resign from the Carlton and free myself from all links with the Conservative Party. This drew me into thinking hard about socialism and doubting the likelihood or desirability of the survival of the social structure. But I did not even qualify as an armchair socialist and I took no steps to join the Labour Party. Above all, I was absorbed by the coming war. In January 1939 I read a paper to Arthur Salter's seminar in All Souls on Europe after Munich in which I predicted that there was nothing to stop the landslide. After Hitler's invasion of Czechoslovakia in March and Mussolini's conquest of Albania in April, I wrongly predicted that the British government would sell Danzig and then the Poles for a further period of so-called peace. Indeed, so confident was I that we were in for a series of Munichs that after a fortnight in camp with the Middlesex Yeomanry at the beginning of August 1939, I set out for Geneva to see an exhibition of pictures from the Prado. Even on 22 August, when my train stopped in Dijon and I heard the astonishing news that Ribbentrop was on his way to Moscow to sign a non-aggression pact with Molotov, my first reaction was to believe that some face-saving formula would be found to keep us out of the war. So I continued the journey to Geneva and spent a whole day concentrating on Goya, Murillo, El Greco, Cranach, Titian and Velasquez. But on my way back to the hotel in the evening I passed by the British Consulate and asked what I should do as a Territorial officer. The reply was to catch the next train home. Even as late as 26 August, on my first day back in London, I was

13

still making the wrong guess that war would be avoided by a last-minute conference and that we would give the whole of Poland away; but after twenty-four hours I could see I was wrong, and when Hitler attacked Poland in the early morning of 1 September I was not even startled by the news. A telephone call summoned me to my regimental headquarters at the Duke of York's Barracks, so I changed into uniform, felt embarrassed by the warm greetings of bystanders in Sloane Square who slapped me on the back shouting 'Good luck, guv'nor', and remained on duty with my regiment until the announcement on 3 September that we were at war: which seemed almost an anticlimax.

I was lucky that at least I had a job to do, in spite of not having in fact even the elementary qualifications to be an officer. I felt ill at ease as the youngest officer in the regiment and was careful not to parade my political views to the others, who were mostly barristers, solicitors or bankers. But as their knowledge of signals and wireless communications was – like mine – the equivalent of nil, I quickly saw that I was no exceptional misfit. The unsettling sense of being in a false position did not last long and I soon found my feet. Another early realization was that a young man's fear of being afraid in wartime was best countered by the surprising boredom of so much of our daily regimental life. An unbelievable amount of time was spent sitting down doing nothing whatever. Ours, in any event, was a regiment so untrained and ill-equipped that half the men in my troop had to bear the indignity of appearing on parade wearing civilian greatcoats – from Montague Burton, the Tailor of Taste – over their battledress. Consequently there was never any question of us being sent to France with the British Expeditionary Force in 1939, and indeed we were not much better trained in the summer of 1940 at the time of Dunkirk and the Battle of Britain. While we prepared that summer for an invasion that mercifully never came, I felt a sense of shame (even if it was no fault of mine) that a full year of war had passed without the experience of any genuinely active service. As the old lags in the regiment kept reminding me, I had not yet heard a shot fired in anger.

In the autumn of 1940 I was posted with a troop of Middlesex Yeomen to the 2nd Royal Horse Artillery (RHA), a highly professional regiment of Regular officers, who did not conceal their scorn for the ignorance and amateurishness of Territorials, beginning with myself. At the end of October we were made part of the 2nd Armoured Division, which left in a convoy from Liverpool and made an arc so wide that we nearly touched Brazil. Finally we disembarked without incident at Suez seven weeks later on Christmas Eve. We were bound for a desert war with the purpose of taking over from the famous 1st Armoured Division, whose early successes in Libya were the first victories of our ground forces since the war began.

We trained hard for three months learning the new art of fighting in the sand. Life in a tent with an occasional weekend in Cairo, where anyone could find a girl, was still virtually peacetime soldiering. I still had not heard a shot fired in anger.

Then in early March 1941 there was a sudden change. General Wavell's victories in North Africa had enabled Anthony Eden to visit Athens in February and offer substantial aid to the Greek government. The decision to find troops for Greece meant that the 2nd Armoured Division was split up. Most of it went to Libya and was in consequence later captured in Rommel's first pushback. If my troop had been amongst them, I would have been a prisoner of war in Italy, like most of the rest of the 2nd Middlesex Yeomanry. The Division, however, sent the 1st Armoured Brigade to Greece in March and I had the luck to be in it, and no less good fortune to emerge without a scratch a month later.

Shipping was so scarce that there were insufficient troop carriers to transport us and we sailed in a millionaire's prewar private steam yacht, built to carry a large house party, which barely survived a savage storm that lasted throughout the three days of our journey from Alexandria to Piraeus. I was violently seasick and scarcely moved from my bunk, wondering if it were possible to imagine a more ignominious end to a brief military career than to be sunk at sea by an act of God. But the sudden warmth that we found on our arrival and the enthusiasm of everyone in Athens, where we spent the evenings treated like heroes – as if we had already won a battle – made the nightmare crossing from Alexandria vanish in a flash. The Brigade then assembled and drove up through Attica and Thessaly, cheered through every town and village and pelted with flowers. The other British forces consisted of the New Zealand Division, under

Major General Freyberg, the 6th Australian Division and eighty RAF aircraft.

In early April the Armoured Brigade occupied a position outside Edessa in the Macedonian plain with a set battle plan to delay the expected German advance. But this plan never worked because, with the crumbling of Yugoslav resistance, it quickly became apparent, after the German invasion began on 6 April with greatly superior forces, that they would come into Greece behind our backs through the Monastir Gap. So we began by being caught on the wrong foot, and the Armoured Brigade was forced to retire and fight the first of a number of delaying actions beginning on 11 April when the 2nd RHA fired over open sights on the 9th Panzer Division and the SS Adolf Hitler Division. It was my first battle experience and I clearly remember how surprised I was that I was not frightened when under fire for the first time. That evening I explained it to myself as the difference between being a witness and a participant in the event. Already by then the RAF had been shot out of the sky and every plane in sight was theirs, not ours. This meant that during our retreat beginning on 17 April we were constantly dive-bombed, but were mercifully spared this experience when crossing a slim bridge over the Aliakmon River where the Luftwaffe carelessly allowed us a clear passage. For the next four days we moved slowly south toward Athens, exchanging turns with our drivers so as to catch an occasional snatch of sleep. There was little serious fighting and of the twenty-six men under my command two were killed by machine-gunning from the air and ten were taken prisoner when part of our retreating convoy was broken up by the Luftwaffe. By 26 April the Armoured Brigade had reached Porto Rafti outside Athens where we destroyed our vehicles and anything else that might have been of use to the enemy, and waited on the beach for the Navy to come and evacuate us with calm and skill. I climbed aboard ship, lugging a wireless set on my back, and slumped into the nearest bunk in such a state of collapse that it was only some hours later that I realized my next-door companion was Julian Oxford, who had been a close university friend before the war. We compared notes on our reactions as we had passed through Thermopylae.

The muddle, confusion and uncertainty which had begun and

continued from the opening day, when the Germans came at us from two directions that we had not anticipated, had provided my long-delayed introduction to the reality of war. It was a bad start, but I had survived and could fight again. A further piece of luck came my way at the first air attack, which broke up our naval convoy and caused part of it to make for Crete. The ship I was in, however, reached Alexandria without mishap and we disembarked in the sunshine. We were all given local leave and I remember my first action was to burn the bug-ridden shirt I had worn for three weeks and then laze in a bath for an hour, wondering whether any Pharaoh had been conscious of such luxury.

On 2 May I wrote to my mother:

I am now safe, healthy, unscathed and all of a piece from Greece after a somewhat alfresco journey to and fro. The battle fighting was enthralling and surprisingly unbloody. Confusion was the dominant factor. I felt less keyed up when fighting than waiting to go in to bat or just before an exam; but general excitement and almost total lack of sleep for days on end, plus a weird river of brandy, whisky and gin have left the nerves a trifle frayed. I dropped nearly all my kit not far from the Acropolis, but managed to salvage a pair of silk pants and two volumes of Plato. I now find that I am one of five officers left in the Middlesex Yeomanry as a large part of the rest of the regiment has been captured by Rommel in Libya.

The only home for those of us who had emerged from Greece was to join the 1st Middlesex Yeomanry in Palestine, where they had been stationed since the end of 1939, complete with their horses, as part of the 1st Cavalry Division. So I joined them in May 1941 and was posted as signals officer to the 6th Cavalry Brigade, which was stationed at Hadera, a small Jewish settlement near Haifa. After the fall of Crete and before Hitler invaded Russia in June, we felt we were in a potential battle area, as it was assumed that the Germans would make parachute landings in Palestine. One of my first assignments was to make contact via the Jewish Agency representative in Hadera with his headquarters in Haifa to see if they would cooperate with us in a communications plan in the event of an invasion. I was surprised by the immediate acceptance of our proposal by Jewish Agency headquarters, and even more so by the calm revelation that all the

17

water towers between Haifa and Jerusalem were already manned by trained teams of Haganah signallers, who had five years' experience of operating a highly efficient communications system by flash lamp against the British. When we organized joint manoeuvres, it was soon discovered that their signals skill exceeded ours. The system was never put to the test because Palestine quickly became a backwater when Hitler plunged into Russia in June 1941.

At the end of that summer I fell ill and was sent to a hospital in Sarafand, near Jerusalem, for a minor operation requiring a long convalescence. It was while I was lying in bed with more than ample time to reflect on what might happen to me when I was released, that I received a sad little letter from the Colonel of my regiment saying that the Middlesex Yeomanry was being disbanded and that henceforth it was each man for himself. He offered no advice, so I had to advise myself. It was then that I decided to write two letters trying to open two different kinds of opportunity. The first was to my former squadron leader in Greece, Major G. W. F. de Winton, whom I knew to be in Tobruk, which was a surrounded enclave but was still holding out. I asked if I could join him in any capacity, not mentioning that I was convalescing from an operation. I got no reply and assumed the letter never reached him.

The other letter was to Major F. Allhusen, with whom I had made friends on the ship travelling out to Suez in 1940. He had served in the same regiment as Anthony Eden at the end of the First World War and was in the process of being posted to Sofia as Military Attaché. Since the Germans took over Bulgaria while our convoy was sailing up the Red Sea, he naturally stayed in Cairo and took up an appointment in Military Intelligence at General Headquarters (GHQ). I had kept in touch with him during the stray occasions that I had been in Cairo, and I therefore knew him well enough to give a frank statement of the position I was in and ask if he could steer me towards an interesting but, above all, an active job. I never heard from him directly and never saw him again in my life. But it was clearly he who must have passed my name down the line, with or without the embroidery which was soon to cause me such surprise.

Shortly thereafter a middle-aged figure of military bearing but in civilian clothes strode briskly down the hospital ward in Sarafand asking if there was anyone of my name. When I had been ushered into a private room, he gave me orders to be seated and said that he had heard from GHQ Cairo that I had volunteered to join MI6, the Secret Intelligence Service (SIS). In view of my exceptional qualifications as a fluent Arabic speaker, he wondered whether I would like to become his assistant in the Embassy in Baghdad, where there was much to be done analysing the political situation in the aftermath of Rashid Ali's pro-Nazi rebellion in April 1941. He claimed that his sources of information had unearthed Rashid Ali's plot in the nick of time and that he carried an important part of the responsibility for assuring the stability of Nuri Pasha's government.

I suppose he saw me looking somewhat bewildered, because he asked me to confirm my name once again before I was given the right to reply. My first question, which he did not answer, was to ask who had given him my name. Then I said that I must immediately clear up two apparent misunderstandings. Far from being a fluent Arabic speaker, I knew no Arabic at all. At Oxford I had read history, not Oriental languages. Secondly, when asking for an active job, I had had no thought of joining the Secret Intelligence Service, about which I knew nothing. But these appeared to him to be minor matters and the offer was repeated to become his assistant as soon as I could be discharged from hospital. When I accepted, his first instruction was that I should buy a dinner jacket.

In this strange way I arrived in Baghdad shortly before Christmas 1941 and spent the next eighteen months sharing Freya Stark's house in Alwiyah. She was already a Middle Eastern celebrity in her own right, and had just started the Iraqi branch of 'The Brothers of Freedom', an organization that she had launched in Aden and Egypt soon after the start of the war, which – with the cooperation of many Iraqi groups throughout the country – successfully spread the word about the positive side of our war aims, as well as providing the arguments why the dictators would be defeated. By lodging with her, I was given the chance to meet the leading actors at the centre of the stage: Prime Minister Nuri Pasha and the members of his government, the Commander-in-Chief, General Wilson, as well as the army of her

British and Iraqi friends who were constantly clustering round her house. It was at first an exciting, carefree prewar life with cocktail parties and black-tie dinners, tennis, golf and horses brought to the door for our morning ride before breakfast.

I also had a job to do, which taught me how an Embassy worked and gave me my first experience of political analysis and the jungle of the intelligence world. There were three rival organizations: the Secret Intelligence Service's office within the Embassy, in which I worked; the Special Operations Executive (SOE), whose main task was to prepare a resistance movement to greet the Germans if we had to abandon Iraq; and the Army's Chief Intelligence Centre Iraq (CICI), where the key posts were held by members of the Security Service (MI5). There was constant bickering and jealousy.

In my early days in Baghdad I had naturally made a point of learning how the three rival organizations, SIS, MI5 and SOE, had come into existence. The head of my office had proudly quoted 1909 as the date of birth of SIS, when the Committee of Imperial Defence had divided intelligence responsibilities between the Security Service (MI5) for the territories of the British Empire and SIS (MI6) for the rest of the world. In the interwar period, responsibility for SIS was shunted between the War Office, the Admiralty and the Foreign Office. From my SOE colleagues, I was told that it was not until 1938, after Hitler had taken over Austria, that Section D of SIS was established under Colonel Laurence Grand to study sabotage, guerrilla activities and subversion against German influence in Europe. At the same time the War Office had started a section that became known as Military Intelligence (Research) or MI(R) to study the techniques of irregular warfare. After the collapse of France, SOE, which absorbed both Section D of SIS and MI(R), was set up under the Ministry of Economic Warfare, then headed by Hugh Dalton, and began to operate with Churchill's inspiring directive to 'set Europe ablaze'.[1] It did not take me long to form my own judgment of the different organizations and their organizers. If I was at first puzzled, I soon became cynical about the time spent

[1] See David Stafford, *Britain and European Resistance 1940-1945* (Macmillan, 1980), and Douglas Dodds-Parker, *Setting Europe Ablaze* (Springwood Books, 1983).

on fierce interdepartmental warfare. It became a commonplace to say that if fifty per cent of the day could be devoted to trying to defeat Hitler, we were doing well and might win the war. The SOE team was unquestionably the best in my view and I collaborated with them closely. This did not always please the head of my office (SIS), who preferred to believe what he was told by his own sources of information, and had restricted his contacts with the rest of the intelligence community to an irreducible minimum. After a year he was replaced by another major from the First World War who lasted a matter of months. When he left in the early summer of 1943, our regional head office in Cairo asked me to take over the Embassy intelligence organization and offered me promotion. They seemed aggrieved when I turned down the job. The simple truth was that I had become restless and increasingly conscious of the illegitimacy of diplomatic life for someone of sound health, aged twenty-six, in a backwater of the war. I knew that I was untrained and unfitted for regimental duties and, in any event, my regiment no longer existed. My only hope of returning to active service was to volunteer for a special mission.

So I wrote to Cairo, backed by a helpful letter of recommendation from the Ambassador, Sir Kinahan Cornwallis, saying that I wanted above all to be sent into Europe to operate behind the lines. The Ambassador's letter, which was indiscreetly shown to me by his private secretary, described me as

a young man who has matured over the past year and learned to express himself, both in discussion and on paper, with greater care and circumspection than when he first arrived. He has acquired an aptitude for political analysis and has plenty of energy which he understandably wishes at his age to devote to more directly thwarting the designs of the King's enemies than by examining the intricacies of Iraqi politics. I wish him well and hope that his energies can be steered to more appropriately active service for someone of his age than is available to him in this Embassy.

I was also advised by my friends in SOE to switch over to their side, and they too wrote to their headquarters in Cairo to support me. The result was a welcome telegram in July 1943 transferring me to Cairo, without delay, but no mention was made of the assignment I was to be given.

On my arrival there was an argument, mild by the standards of those days, as to who should employ me. I felt somewhat flattered by the contest over my body, which ended with a smiling reprimand for 'my disloyalty in cultivating such close relations with SOE' – this was indeed a foretaste of what was to come – but it ended amicably with instructions to report to the Yugoslav office of SIS, which offered me the opportunity of being dropped by parachute to Tito and operating as part of Bill Deakin's mission. By a quirk of circumstance, I had got to know him quite well in my last year at Oxford when he was a don at Wadham, and had attended his lectures. I accepted the job with alacrity. This was a quicker decision than I had expected and more than fulfilled all my hopes of getting back into the thick of things.

I bought a Serbo-Croat grammar and phrase book, read every report available about Tito and flew off in a matter of days to Ramat David in Palestine, where a parachute school had been organized to provide the minimum training necessary for people like myself to land in one piece. I shared a tent with two Yugoslavs of different political persuasions, whose arguments taught me a good deal about the problems Tito was confronting. One of them was to be my wireless operator and we were due to drop together. A fairly rigorous physical training course had been arranged to toughen us up. I was as scared as everyone else on all four practice jumps, but like everyone else I survived and went back to Cairo with no other thought in my mind but to hope that I would not be kept waiting for long. After brief instruction in identifying German military formations and in the elementary handling of sabotage material, I was sent to SOE to meet Hugh Seton-Watson, who packed into an hour a brilliant exposition of how and why British support had switched from Mihailovic to Tito.[2] There was, however, time for no more extensive briefing, as I was told that speed was all that mattered. Indeed everything seemed set, when we heard that Fitzroy Maclean had joined Tito in September as Churchill's personal representative. Not long after, my wireless operator and I flew to Tokra in Libya, with a mixed group of others from SOE on different missions.

At Tokra there was the normal delay and anticlimax. First one

[2] See F. W. D. Deakin, *The Embattled Mountain* (Oxford University Press, 1971), and Fitzroy Maclean, *Eastern Approaches* (Jonathan Cape, 1949).

of the planes was out of action. Then the weather reports were unfavourable and one of the pilots fell sick. We sat about getting fidgety and irritable. Finally we were told one morning over breakfast that our operation would take place that night. I thought I had made it at last. We had an hour's practice with our despatcher in the early evening, followed by a good dinner and the final fitting of our parachutes. Indeed, we actually climbed into the plane and ran through the drill of an operational jump.

There had been a rumour in the mess (where all the talk was rumour) that the latest weather report would cancel our flight that night, but I had thought no more of it when we were told to embark. We sat in the aircraft for what seemed a suspiciously long time. Eventually a prim RAF officer poked his head in and said we were to return to the mess for further instructions. There I was told that there had been a last-minute change in the weather report and that further maintenance was needed on our plane.

Neither my wireless operator nor I believed either of those stories. I remember storming out of the mess in a rage and cursing the sky. The next morning nothing happened and I had a strong premonition that the whole adventure had collapsed. Soon there was total confirmation of the worst of my fears as the Yugoslav office sent me the following message from Cairo on 18 September: 'Tito has refused to accept further personnel and asks for stores only. Have pointed out that you are bringing wireless sets which cannot be despatched without you. Deakin is making further approaches. Will keep you informed.'

I did not allow myself to hope that there would be any abrupt change in the situation, and when I read the telegram to my wireless operator, he said bluntly that he had had enough and wanted to return to Cairo. I agreed with him and said so. The whole thing seemed a fraud. Then I decided to telephone to Cairo and in highly emotional language asked what was going on. I remember the embarrassed reply, which made me suspect that I was not being given the true story. In any event, I was told that we should both return to Cairo on the next available plane.

In fact, as I soon learned, I had been given the true story. Indeed, in retrospect, Tito's line can easily be understood. But at the time I had a furiously different view on both scores. On my return, the Yugoslav office in Cairo offered me the usual expressions of sympathy and told me to calm down, be patient and wait my turn. It might be a month or two, they said, before the situation became clearer. I commented that it might be longer and challenged them to disagree. This was followed by an argument at cross purposes. Then an ill-timed proposal was made that I might like a staff job in Algiers. To this I replied that I insisted on getting into Europe somewhere and somehow. I did not mind where or how, but the sooner the better. I think my point was quickly taken, because in a matter of days I was told to report to the Greek office. It seemed that something odd had just taken place in north-western Greece which might give me a chance of being dropped in quickly. I said goodbye to my Yugoslav wireless operator and never saw him again. My Yugoslav adventure ended in a flat anticlimax.

At the start of my interview with the head of the Greek office of SIS, I could see straightaway that he was embarrassed by the proposition that he was to put to me. Doodling with his pencil on a writing pad and not looking me in the face, he spoke jerkily, searching for his words, unable to express himself with conviction. I was at first given some random observations on the general difficulties he had experienced in working with SOE, both in Cairo and in Greece. They were a funny lot, he said, and sometimes one wondered whose side they were on. In any event, they were up to their eyes in 'the political business', as he kept on calling it, and which, after some innocent questions from me, was translated to mean the differing politics of a sharply divided resistance movement.[3] While I was wondering in what direction this disjointed discourse would lead us, he mentioned he had just been given the shocking news that SOE had shot his main agent in Epirus, claiming that he was a traitor in touch with the Germans. I was told this man was an American Greek, running under the name of Costa Lawrence, whose reports had covered most of north-western Greece since he had been infiltrated into the area in late 1942. After further embarrassed pauses, I was asked if I would be prepared to take Lawrence's place. My answer was given before the formal offer was made, as acceptance solved my main problem of getting into Europe quickly and expunging

[3] See C. M. Woodhouse, *Apple of Discord* (Hutchinson, 1948) and *The Struggle for Greece* (Hart Davis, MacGibbon, 1976).

my unhappy experience with the Yugoslav office. I was so excited by the prospect of a new adventure that it did not occur to me at that stage to make even superficial inquiries about the circumstances of Lawrence's disappearance from the scene. This was apparently construed as a point in my favour, as the head of the Greek office became more relaxed as soon as he discovered that he had found Lawrence's replacement without any difficulty. He then said that two Greeks had already been earmarked to join my mission, which was being organized at the special request of GHQ in Cairo to report on the German order of battle in professional detail. GHQ was in close liaison with both SIS and SOE as well as with the Greek government in exile. Military intelligence, I was told, had been brushed aside by SOE as a secondary or even tertiary consideration in the course of their absorption with the politics of the Greek Resistance. In consequence far too little was known about 'the real enemy', and I was given the first of many repeated instructions to keep my nose out of politics, concentrate on the main objective, maintain the good reputation of the service with the Foreign Office and not meddle in matters which should properly be handled by the Foreign Office and not by SOE. This was plainly not the moment to ask what lay behind such accusations, and I was in any case so elated at the prospect of starting a new adventure that I welcomed the quick closure of the interview and the arrangements to meet my new Greek colleagues.

Soon afterwards I was introduced to Lieutenant Vassilis Kalousis, who was a regular Greek army officer of about my age, and Sergeant Giorgos Katsikakis, who was to be our wireless operator. As neither of them had done their parachute training we all three went back to Palestine and I did the whole course again a second time. We shared a tent and were helped by these circumstances to get to know one another and act as a team. Kalousis spoke some French, so we had a means of communication; but I took this opportunity of plunging into a study of Greek and urging them both to teach me their language. A parachute course is a tense experience and I could not disguise the fact that I felt no less scared than my colleagues at each practice jump. But although we all started as strangers to one another, and the relationship between Kalousis and Katsikakis kept them at the

25

normal distance between a subaltern and a sergeant, the stiffness had worn off by the end of the course and we were ready to work as a group. Kalousis was a quiet-spoken, determined, well-disciplined officer with a sense of humour. He came from Himara in northern Epirus as he called it, or southern Albania as it was shown on the map. Katsikakis hailed from the island of Samos near the coast of Turkey. He was full of fun and gaiety, sharing the deep curiosity of his countrymen about all foreigners. I quickly learned that 'foreign' in Greek covered both myself and Kalousis, as London and Himara were approximately equidistant from Samos in his estimate. While I struggled to produce simple sentences in Greek and welcomed their insistence on correcting every mistake, I could see from the quick patter of their dialogue late into the night and their winks and smiles during the day that they were establishing a satisfactory working relationship between themselves and were sharing the amuse-ment of the experience of serving under a British officer. Somewhat to my surprise, I was not closely questioned by Kalousis about the political situation in Greece, and as I was myself at this juncture profoundly ignorant of what was going on, it was a relief not to undergo an interrogation from which I could only have emerged with shame. As I was only beginning to learn their language, I could not follow their political discussions except in the broadest outline, but at the end of a long gossip, Kalousis would courteously give me a summary in French to prevent my being left out in the cold. By the time we returned to Cairo, I knew no more than that both my colleagues were fiercely anti-Communist and held generally supportive views about the King and the exiled Greek government in Egypt. But I had also realized that even if I were to obey my instructions to keep out of the political business, it would be essential to brief myself on the background to the politics of the resistance, and I innocently anticipated that I would be helped in this connection by the Greek office.

When we reached Cairo, Kalousis and Katsikakis were taken in hand by the Greek office, while I spent most of a week at GHQ being closely briefed by military intelligence officers on the detailed information they required on the strength, location, mobility, equipment, efficiency and morale of the German units in western Greece and southern Albania under the command of Lieutenant General Hubert Lanz. I was instructed to pay particular attention to the identification of units of the XXII Mountain Corps, the names of the commanding officers and the organization of Lanz's headquarters in Ioannina, his movements and those of his Chief of Staff. Importance was also attached to covering the military traffic movements along the main roads north, south, east and west of Ioannina. Lanz was known to have recently taken command of this area, but I was told that virtually none of the detailed information GHQ required to construct the German order of battle, which would be opposing an Allied landing, had been provided by SOE. Although no mention was made of Costa Lawrence, I could only assume that whatever else he had done, he had not been reporting the military intelligence needed by GHQ. In the event of German prisoners or deserters coming my way, I was briefed how to examine their paybooks for leads in interrogation, and I was given a copy of a captured German handbook with which it would be simple to identify German units and formations from their vehicle signs. When I had satisfied myself that I knew what was required of my mission, I retailed my briefing to Kalousis, speaking in French, and discussed with him and others in the Greek office the kind of contacts he hoped to make when he had infiltrated himself into Ioannina.

At GHQ I had been given a scanty outline of the two main parts of the Greek resistance movement, which were known by their Greek acronyms: EAM/ELAS (National Liberation Front/National Popular Liberation Army), which were the political and military arms, respectively, of the movement that controlled most of mountain Greece, except in Epirus. This part of western Greece was held by EDES (National Republican Greek League), EAM/ELAS's main rival, commanded by Napoleon Zervas. These names had in fact been mentioned to me by Kalousis during the parachute course and he had added one more set of initials to the list, KKE (Communist Party of Greece), which he claimed was the driving force behind EAM/ELAS. He had also informed me that ELAS and EDES were in a state of civil war. This was, of course, confirmed to me in GHQ, with the wry comment that perhaps it explained why SOE, with missions to both sides of the civil war, had not been able to focus their attention on 'the real enemy', and why practically nothing was known about the German order of battle.

When the Greek office sent me alone to SOE headquarters in Cairo, it had already been agreed that my mission – code name 'Jute' – consisting of Kalousis, Katsikakis and myself would be dropped in Epirus and formally attached to SOE's Allied Military Mission under Lieutenant Colonel Tom Barnes at EDES headquarters. Once again I was warned in advance to be on my guard and not to express any political opinions, and it was stressed that my objectives were strictly confined to the acquisition of the military intelligence required by GHQ. I spent an entertaining few days in an atmosphere more reminiscent of a newspaper office than of a paramilitary headquarters. I found myself talking to people who were politically alert and whose judgments, right or wrong, were persuasively argued. In one room I heard a panegyric of Zervas and in another an anathema against him. In the space of a day, he was described as a national hero, as well as an untrustworthy ruffian with a colourful but disreputable political past whose 'splinter group', EDES, had divided an otherwise united 'democratic resistance movement'. Before such voluble briefing, it was easy to obey my instructions 'to listen and not to talk'. But although I welcomed every scrap of information that was offered to me, it was difficult to piece together so much contradictory evidence. A further problem was what to reveal and what not to reveal to Kalousis, who had an entirely legitimate interest in sharing whatever information I was gathering. During the parachute course, we had agreed that it would be unwise to jump to conclusions and more prudent to form judgments of the political situation once we had arrived. I therefore sidestepped his questions about the impressions I had gained of Zervas's reputation and standing in SOE.

When I told the head of the Greek office of the confusing accounts I had been given at SOE and how the situation should be presented to Kalousis, he merely shrugged his shoulders and repeated his set speech about keeping out of the political business and concentrating on the Germans as the main enemy and my only target. My first duty, he unhelpfully emphasized, was to escape the fate of Costa Lawrence. I must avoid, if conceivably possible, any open breach with SOE on any issue; but at the same time my mission was to be kept separate from all their activities, and I was given a string of assurances that if I obeyed my instructions, I could count on the support of the Greek office within and beyond the limits of what was possible.

When the head of the Greek office referred me upward to his superiors at SIS headquarters in Cairo, which was designated the Inter Services Liaison Department (ISLD), I found myself being interviewed by Army, Navy and Air Force officers who, for different reasons, had left their respective services before the war. Their whole professional upbringing had schooled them to treat politics as an arcane subject, best left to others. Every senior officer to whom I spoke emphasized, sometimes with undisguised pleasure, that SOE 'had made a mess of it' in Greece and this was the root cause of its turbulent relations with the Foreign Office and with the British Embassy to the exiled Greek government in Cairo. I was told that the Ambassador, Rex Leeper, was an enemy of SOE, but when I gently inquired what SOE had done to cause his enmity, the answers I received made me none the wiser. Moreover, the suggestion that I should myself call on the Embassy was politely turned aside. It therefore seemed all the more strange and contradictory to be reminded that SIS came under the Foreign Office, was both shielded by it and should be its shield against 'amateur policy-makers' – as the head of ISLD described them – whose professionalism had been lost when SOE had been allowed to break away from SIS in the summer of 1940 and set up on its own under the aegis of the Ministry of Economic Warfare.

Now that I had tested it out at different levels, I could see more clearly than in Baghdad that the child, SOE, had outgrown its parent, SIS. Even from my brief contacts with SOE it was clear that both their military and civilian members were of a quite different stamp. They had no fear whatever of trading in political commodities and knew that resistance in Europe was as political a matter as the composition of a government. Hence, in this respect SOE outgunned SIS for the simple reason that SIS had virtually no artillery. As usual, personalities also had their part to play in the rivalry between the two organizations in Cairo, which were in effect at loggerheads with one another.

Though I was not to know it at the time, the rivalry between SOE and SIS was no less fierce in London, with one vital difference. The head of SIS, Sir Stewart Menzies, operating both from his office in Broadway and his club, White's in St James's Street, was closer to the levers of power than any of his rivals and exploited to the full his direct access to the Prime Minister. He was greatly helped by Major Desmond Morton, who had been a trusted adviser to Churchill before the war while he was serving in SIS and had naturally graduated into Churchill's inner circle after 1940. No one in his right mind would have accused Menzies of being outgunned in Whitehall. But SIS's position in London was in no way reflected in the power and influence of ISLD, its regional headquarters in Cairo.

When therefore I tiptoed forward with some elementary inquiries about the politics of mountain Greece, which I would shortly be experiencing, at no level in ISLD were answers available to the following questions. Was His Majesty's Government (HMG) irrevocably committed to support the King's return to Greece after liberation? How did the exiled Greek government in Cairo maintain its links with the Resistance? What did EDES and Zervas represent? If it was true, as I had been told by Kalousis, that Zervas had a republican past, when and how had he come to terms with the King? Or was he opposed to the King's return? Obviously EAM/ELAS was, by definition, republican; but was it partly or wholly under Communist control? In any event, what was the role of the Greek Communist Party? What were EAM/ELAS's links with Tito? On what issue and how and when had fighting broken out between EDES and ELAS? Which of the two had been the first to organize resistance? Which had done the most damage to the Germans?

These, one might have thought, were no more than the normal questions likely to be asked by any newcomer to the scene. I had hoped for brief, standard, textbook answers, but whenever I alluded to these matters, I was told again and again that I did not need this kind of information and should be concentrating all my efforts on the buildup and analysis of the German order of battle. The impression left on me at the end of my briefing in ISLD was that Lanz might have been operating, not within and part of a civil war, but across a sparsely populated desert.

The background to 'the political business', which I had no means of learning at the time, was that sporadic resistance had started not long after I had been evacuated from Greece in April 1941. In the following September the National Liberation Front (EAM) had been founded by the Greek Communist Party (KKE), although EAM was careful not to parade this fact in its early days. The National Liberation Front was a well-chosen, non-political name carefully designed to draw all and sundry under its wing. When, however, EAM's representatives put out feelers to some of the leading political figures in prewar Athens, they failed to attract to their cause either a dynamic Populist (Conservative) like Panayiotis Kanellopoulos or such Liberals as George Papandreou, the father of Andreas (who became Prime Minister in 1981), or Themistocles Sophoulis, all of whom had been victims of Metaxas's dictatorship, imposed on 4 August 1936 with the sanction of King George II. The King had returned to Greece in November 1935 after nearly twelve years in exile and as a direct result of a 'fixed' plebiscite. He had thereupon appointed a caretaker government (dominated by extreme royalists) to supervise the next elections. While granting an amnesty to his political opponents, King George firmly refused to reinstate republican (mostly Venizelist) officers in the Army.

Following the 1936 elections, which had produced a stalemated Chamber of Deputies equally divided between Populists (royalists) and Liberals (Venizelists/republicans) and ostensibly in order to forestall an attempt by the Communists to foment labour unrest and civil strife, Ioannis Metaxas, who had been appointed by the King to the Ministry of War in March 1936, found fortunate pretexts in the strikes of the ensuing summer and the electoral agreements between the Communists and the Liberals, to seize power himself in a coup d'état on 4 August 1936. Hitherto, although well known as a staunch monarchist, Metaxas had been no more than a minor political figure. His reputation rested on his military career, which had begun as a student at the War College in Berlin. He became Chief of Staff in the Balkan Wars of 1912-13, and supported the pro-German stance of King Constantine in the First World War. After his coup and with the King's approval, a state of martial law was proclaimed, the constitution was suspended and parliament was dissolved. For the next four and a half years, Greece was ruled by a dictatorship.

Although the Foreign Office had at first little liking or respect for Metaxas, he became the second most trusted friend of HMG in Greece after King George, on whom British policy pivoted.[4] Surprisingly, in view of his earlier fascist leanings and the plainly fascist character of his regime, Metaxas's courageous answer 'No' to Mussolini's impossible demands, which brought Greece into the war in October 1940, made him an instant (if only temporary) hero. The start of the Italo-Albanian war opened and quickly closed an epic chapter in Greek history. By the time Metaxas died suddenly in January 1941, the British Embassy in Athens and the Foreign Office – but certainly not his political opponents in Greece who had suffered exile and many worse indignities – had forgotten their earlier reservations on his political behaviour. The Greek Army's achievements against Mussolini in Albania and King George's unflinching support of HMG to the bitter end of the German invasion in April 1941 understandably made both Churchill and the Foreign Office, who were at one on this issue, hope that the King would be restored to his throne in a liberated Greece. Indeed the King's return was widely interpreted to be the primary objective of British policy and the governing factor in Anglo-Greek relations with the King's exiled government in Cairo.

Such a policy stance cut across the traditionally Anglophile attitude of many of the Liberal politicians themselves which went back at least to the events of 1916-17, when Eleftherios Venizelos forcibly switched the pro-German position of King Constantine and declared war on the Central Powers. The monarchy continued to be a profoundly divisive issue in Greek life through Greece's Anatolian adventure (1919-22) and the whole of the period between the two world wars; it was no less divisive after the German occupation of continental Greece in April 1941 and the subsequent air attack on Crete, when Greeks began to escape

[4] See John Koliopoulos, *Greece and the British Connection, 1935-1944* (Oxford University Press, 1977).

to the Middle East by land and sea to carry on the struggle, by whatever means, as Britain's allies. The news they brought out in 1941 and 1942 in no way surprised the SOE specialists who had a good political understanding of prewar Greece (in contrast to their counterparts in SIS). All their reports stressed that whatever resistance of any serious character had been organized against the Germans was the work of confirmed anti-monarchists, and that there was increasingly widespread support for the position that the restoration of the monarchy should be put to the people's vote by an honest plebiscite. Some reports went so far as to claim that their determination to fight the common enemy was dependent on an undertaking that the King's return would not be in any way imposed on the country, once it had been liberated.

Fortuitously, EDES had also been founded in September 1941, in the same month as EAM, by two prewar republican figures with military backgrounds, Stylianos Gonatas and Napoleon Zervas. Both owed allegiance to EDES's political head, General Nicholaos Plastiras, who had been living in France, in exile on Metaxas's orders, since 1936. All three had committed EDES to oppose the King's return after liberation without a plebiscite. Moreover, Emmanuel Tsouderos, the Prime Minister of the exiled Greek government in Cairo, had received a letter from Gonatas toward the end of 1941 claiming that all the political leaders remaining in Athens regarded the King as deprived of his throne in consequence of Metaxas's dictatorship. In origin, therefore, EDES was no less republican than EAM. The main political message emerging from occupied Greece was therefore unmistakably plain: that resistance to the German occupation had became a republican monopoly. Consequently, there would be fierce opposition to the King's return without a plebiscite. This did not square with official British policy and naturally led to early suspicions in the Foreign Office that SOE was guilty of twisting the facts. It was neither the first nor the last time that an intelligence assessment presenting unpopular news brought discredit on its originators.

Although there had been much talk of serious armed resistance in occupied Greece at the start of 1942, it had failed to materialize until the early summer when Aris Velouchiotis, an avowed Communist, began in May to operate with a small band of ELAS guerrillas in Roumeli, the mountainous strip of territory to the north of the Gulf of Corinth. In July 1942 Zervas was persuaded – indeed pushed – by SOE contacts to slip out of Athens, where he was being closely watched by the Germans, and start EDES as an additional guerrilla movement in southern Epirus. This was his home country, and he was quickly able to raise sufficient followers to begin operations designed to interrupt the Italian communication route from Albania, through Ioannina and Arta, to Athens. On 30 September 1942 the first SOE parachute landing, led by Brigadier Eddie Myers, a regular officer in the Royal Engineers, and C. M. Woodhouse, took place in Roumeli.

Their first objective was to organize a plan, with the assistance of whatever elements could be mobilized from the Greek resistance (about which very little was known), in order to destroy the Gorgopotamos viaduct across which the main railway ran bringing supplies from the north of Greece to Piraeus and thence to reinforce Rommel in North Africa. GHQ in Cairo had originally planned this strategic operation to support the advance of the Eighth Army, which began at El Alamein on 23 October; but by the time it took place, General Montgomery was well on his way. The delay had been due to Aris's deliberate avoidance of contact with Woodhouse – in sharp contrast to Zervas, who immediately agreed to cooperate. Once Aris heard that Zervas would participate in the Gorgopotamos operation, he abruptly changed course and also agreed to cooperate, in order to prevent Zervas from claiming exclusive credit if the operation proved to be successful. In fact it was a complete success. On 25 November Zervas, Aris and the SOE team, acting in concert and following the plan worked out by Myers, destroyed the viaduct. This was the first and last time that ELAS and EDES cooperated in a major operation. It showed the military potential of Greek guerrillas and was the first evidence that Greek resistance had a serious contribution to make to the Allied war effort. It established Zervas's organization. Indeed, it was Zervas's willingness to cooperate which forced Aris to join in at the last moment. If Zervas had not made the first move, it is virtually certain that Aris would have continued to keep his distance from Myers and Woodhouse, the Gorgopotamos viaduct would not have been destroyed and the history of the Greek resistance would have got away to a very different start.

If the skill and courage of all concerned in this operation revealed to GHQ in Cairo the advantages of a cooperative resistance movement, it did not persuade the Foreign Office at that stage that Greek guerrilla forces, regardless of their left-wing (ELAS) or right-wing (EDES) labels, were a factor to be entered in the political audit. This was the start of the conflict of priorities between the Chiefs of Staff (and their military planners) and the Foreign Office, whose first requirement was to secure the future position of the King against both anti-royalist resistance movements. For some months after the Gorgopotamos operation in November 1942, the Foreign Office took the view that both ELAS and EDES were little better than bandit organizations of comparable disrepute. If an open mind was kept on allegations that EAM was dominated by the Greek Communist Party and that ELAS was controlled by EAM and was itself consequently under Communist direction, this did nothing to advantage Zervas. His links with the republican stance of General Plastiras and the constant emphasis on the need for a plebiscite before the King could return, made the Foreign Office rate EDES as bad, if not worse than, ELAS. This political appreciation made a misfit with the current requirements of Anglo-American strategy. The decision to invade Sicily had been taken at Casablanca in January 1943, which meant that there was an important role for Greek resistance to play – namely to tie down as many enemy troops as possible and to deceive the German High Command into believing that there would be an Allied landing in the Balkans.

For the first three months of 1943 SOE was receiving an overlapping and conflicting series of reports from Myers, Woodhouse and Rufus Sheppard – who had been dropped on Mount Olympus unknown to Myers. Since neither Myers nor Woodhouse had received any political briefing in Cairo, they did not know that in their perceptive and accurate reports on Zervas's republican views, on EAM's intentions to frustrate a genuine plebiscite at the end of the war if it would advantage Plastiras, and on Communist control of the EAM Central Committee, five members of which Woodhouse had met on a clandestine visit to Athens, they were giving a version of events near the opposite of what the Foreign Office would wish to hear. This was merely the start of the confusion. It was increased by Sheppard's performance. He seemed to swallow EAM propaganda without a qualm by reporting that it was a broadly based movement whose pro-British leaders even understood the need to recognize the King. To make the confusion more confounded, the Foreign Office did not at that stage know how the diplomatic hand was being played in mountain Greece and SOE had not been able to reconcile the conflicting reports it was receiving on EAM.

In early February 1943, two more republican officers arrived in the mountains to establish their own independent guerrilla bands. Unlike Zervas, Colonel Stephanos Saraphis and Colonel Dimitrios Psarros had good prewar reputations. The latter, operating separately but in parallel with EDES in the area of Mount Parnassos, formed a group which soon styled itself EKKA (National and Social Liberation). Inevitably, both Saraphis and Psarros were in competition with ELAS, which quickly took action by surrounding Saraphis's group in Thessaly and taking him prisoner in early March. This manoeuvre paid off handsomely, since Saraphis soon switched his allegiance and changed his status from ELAS's prisoner to become its Commander-in-Chief. To Myers and Zervas this was a plain signal of the possibility of civil war between the guerrilla groups and destroyed the hopes of establishing 'national bands', which had recently been discussed between Saraphis and Zervas. The attack on Saraphis and its consequence was the first event that led to a reconsideration of Zervas by the British authorities.

The second event was Zervas's reaction to a message, which came to his notice in February 1943, from the King's government to loyal officers, warning them against EDES as well as ELAS. He had already experienced ELAS's first aggressive move against EDES shortly after the Gorgopotamos operation, which provided early evidence of EAM/ELAS's intention to monopolize the resistance movement. This objective had been set at the Communist Party's 'Panhellenic Conference' in December 1942 along with the decisions to infiltrate and control the Greek forces in Egypt and to destory the reputation of the King and the exiled Greek government. In consequence, Zervas was now ready to revise his priorities and rate Communism as a greater danger to the country than the monarchy, notably in view of Churchill's full support of the King. The opportunity to demonstrate his changed position came in response to a suggestion from Woodhouse that he might wish to send a friendly message to the King on Greek Independence Day, 25 March. The key sentences in his telegram, sent on 9 March, were more than friendly and showed a policy switch on the vital constitutional question:

If the King returns here as the result of the free opinion expressed by our people, we will be the first to welcome him and consider Greek constitutional quarrels ended. If England for wider reasons and even without the people's wishes wants the return of the King, we, fighting for liberation will not oppose it.[5]

Characteristically, Zervas revealed this radical change of position to none of his immediate entourage and least of all to his second-in-command, Komninos Pyromaglou, whom he rightly assessed to be a hardline republican. But even this dramatic change of front by Zervas did not immediately endear him to the Foreign Office, whose suspicions of his political 'unreliability' continued throughout the summer of 1943, and were nurtured by Ambassador Leeper's growing opposition to the political assessments emerging from SOE which favoured the republican cause. In June 1943, when SOE put up a plan to arrange for Plastiras's escape from France, the Foreign Office turned it down. Leeper, in particular, took the view that Myers had no political aptitude and was meddling dangerously in internal Greek affairs, which were none of his business – notably in his persistent claim that both ELAS and EDES, while violently opposed on virtually every other issue, agreed that the question of the King's return should be decided by a plebiscite.

In May and June 1943 ELAS made two attacks on Colonel Psarros's EKKA. This merely reinforced the Foreign Office's opinion that politically insignificant fratricide was all that could be expected of Greek guerrillas. The event, however, which caused a reassessment in the Foreign Office of the dangers of Greek Communism was the evidence, provided in a report by the Security Service (MI5) in May 1943, that the mutiny in the Greek armed forces in Egypt, which had taken place two months earlier, had been instigated by exfiltrated members of EAM. When SOE

[5] See C. M. Woodhouse, 'EAM and the British Connection' in *Greece in the 1940s*, edited by John O. Iatrides (University Press of New England, 1981).

37

learned of this report from the Foreign Office, it was at a time when Myers was responding to the requirement for diversionary operations to encourage the Germans to believe that the Allied landing would come in Greece and not in Sicily. He was faced with the unpopular task of explaining to his superiors that if Zervas was important because he controlled one of the areas of Greece which the Germans thought would most likely be used for an Allied landing, he nevertheless had no power outside Epirus. Hence the continued Allied dependence on involving ELAS – for the necessary impact of a make-believe countrywide operation – in spite of the political dangers presented by EAM. In fact, when the Allied landings took place in Sicily in July 1943, two German divisions had been sent to the wrong address.

In June 1943 Anthony Eden decided to send in an emissary of his own choice to report personally to him on the situation in the Greek mountains. He picked on David Wallace (his father, Captain Euan Wallace, had been a member of Churchill's government), who had served as Press Attaché at the British Embassy in Athens from the outbreak of war until the evacuation of Greece in April 1941. At the end of June Wallace, with the temporary rank of major – although technically a member of Leeper's Embassy in Cairo – was parachuted into Greece. He served as Myers's political adviser until they jointly succeeded in bringing out to Cairo on 10 August a delegation of leaders drawn from all three of the major resistance movements, EAM/ELAS, EDES and EKKA. But before this important event Wallace had sent out to Leeper, over SOE's wireless channels, a series of reports which generally squared with what Myers and Wood-house had been saying on Communist influence over EAM and on the need to clarify the King's position. These reports did not reach Leeper until twelve days after Wallace had arrived in Cairo, which Leeper construed as further evidence of SOE's devious behaviour and SOE explained as administrative incompetence. It appears that, after his arrival, Wallace made two further points: that SOE had greatly exaggerated the military performance and potential of the guerrilla forces, and that Zervas had been forced against his will and better judgment by Myers to sign the National Bands Agreement in July 1943 which established the Joint General Headquarters (JGHQ) at Pertouli in the

Pindus Mountains. This, in Zervas's view, advantaged EAM/ELAS. The JGHQ disintegrated in October at the start of the 'First Round' of the Greek Civil War. In any event, Leeper's mistrust and disapproval of Myers were further deepened after their encounters in Cairo.

The delegation of resistance leaders[6] consisted of four EAM representatives, Andreas Tzimas, Petros Roussos, Costas Despotopoulos and Ilias Tsirimokos (of whom the first three were Communists); the EDES representative Komninos Pyromaglou, Zervas's second-in-command; and George Kartalis, a prewar Populist turned republican, who spoke for Psarros's EKKA, which was operating separately but in parallel with EDES. Leeper, in particular, did not expect that he would be dealing with men of considerable political sophistication. He was therefore more than disagreeably surprised when the delegation presented a document to Tsouderos, the Prime Minister of the Greek government in exile, calling for an authoritative statement that the King would not return to Greece without a plebiscite. On this issue Pyromaglou and Kartalis, who had good reason to oppose the Communists on every other matter and who knew from personal experience of the threat that they posed, spoke with even greater vigour than the EAM representatives. The delegates also claimed three seats in the Tsouderos government – the Ministries of Interior, Justice and War. (In retrospect, it is of interest that in the short-lived coalition governments which were established in Eastern Europe after liberation, these three Ministries were always the main Communist targets.) The King did not yield, however; he did not have to negotiate his position as he was unconditionally supported by both Churchill and Roosevelt, who were then attending the Quebec Conference. Nor, of course, did Tsouderos wish to give up three important portfolios to any guerrillas. The delegation returned to Greece in mid September 1943 with nothing to show for their efforts, but without Myers. Both Leeper and the Foreign Office persisted in their belief that he had been playing a political role of his own in Greece and had been bamboozled by EAM. It was also held against him that he had put the resistance leaders up to demanding portfolios in the

[6] See Phyllis Auty and Richard Clogg, edd., *British Policy towards Wartime Resistance in Yugoslavia and Greece* (Macmillan, 1975).

Greek government. These misjudgements of Myers were not shared by the Commander-in-Chief, General Wilson, but Churchill took steps to ensure that Myers was formally relieved of his post in November 1943.

During the previous month the 'First Round' of the Greek Civil War had begun in earnest – the direct result of the failure of the resistance delegation to achieve any concrete results in Cairo. Fighting, instigated by ELAS, had broken out between ELAS and EDES in Epirus and between ELAS and other smaller non-Communist guerrilla groups in Macedonia and the Peloponneses. The fact that ELAS attacked its rivals simultaneously all over Greece showed the range of its control, as well as its powers of coordination, in both of which it far surpassed EDES. ELAS could probably count at this time on a force of some 15,000 men, which was between two and three times the size of EDES and vastly outnumbered EKKA's forces, which barely reached four figures. ELAS, furthermore, had skilfully acquired most of the small arms and ammunition, mountain artillery, mortars and machine guns of the Italian Pinerolo Division, based in Thessaly, after it had changed sides following Mussolini's fall and the new Italian government's call for an armistice in August 1943. This reinforcement proved specially valuable to ELAS both in its attacks on EDES and in its ability to resist the German forces, which wisely chose this moment to make telling thrusts against both resistance groups. Heavy casualties were inflicted on both ELAS and EDES, and from mid October to mid November 1943 Zervas was fighting on two fronts. But although he lost some territory in Epirus, he survived.

I was only able to piece together the outline of this story once I had landed in Greece. In Cairo, none of it was revealed to me. I was not told of the Gorgopotamos operation, nor did I know the names of Myers, Woodhouse or Wallace. I was not put in touch with the British Embassy to the Greek government, and I knew precisely nothing of the delegation from the three resistance movements to Cairo in August. I could guess, but I was not told, of the importance of the constitutional question and the role of the King. In fact, this was the key issue, as I was soon to learn. On the other hand, all my briefing centred on the imperative need to steer clear of all SOE's activities and not become involved in any of their political commitments. In any case, the politics of the Resistance was a side show by which I should not be distracted. The main target, so far as I was concerned, was the German order of battle, of which so little was known, because SOE's reports on it were claimed to be amateurish. It was emphasized, till I was sick of hearing it, that the prime purpose of my mission was to professionalize our military intelligence on the Germans, and it was added that I would naturally be held responsible for keeping my team, Kalousis and Katsikakis, in line with these instructions and free of any involvement with SOE.

From all this it was palpably clear to me that mistrust in SIS of SOE was much deeper in Cairo than had been evident even from my experience in Baghdad. I was also beginning to become embarrassed and disturbed by the fact that Kalousis and Katsikakis had been pressing me with questions not dissimilar from those to which I had myself failed to find answers. When I stalled in my replies, my unconvincing performance did little to increase their respect for either myself or those whose orders we were due to carry out. It was therefore a relief to all of us when the signal came for our departure in mid December 1943.

Shortly before leaving, I was promoted to captain and given a false name, Jim Russell. When I innocently asked the purpose of the pseudonym, I was told that it was a matter of principle that I was not allowed to question. This I accepted as a harmless form of make-believe, and held back my comment that if in fact I had landed in Yugoslavia some two months earlier, I would have been living there under my own name. I was also told that SOE in Greece was known as MO4, but that its officers were not required to change their identities. It therefore seemed all the more curious that Kalousis and Katsikakis were allowed to keep their real names.

It had been arranged with SOE headquarters that we would be dropped near a village called Plaisia in the mountains south-east of Ioannina, the capital of Epirus, where a reception party would be awaiting us. Thereafter my orders were to take the first opportunity of meeting Tom Barnes, the head of the Allied Military Mission, who was to be my titular boss, and Zervas, in order to explain to both of them the purpose of my mission.

When I asked for guidance as to what I should say about Costa Lawrence, I was told to feign ignorance. I was given final instructions in the use of a simple letter transposition code to be used for all my operational reports sent by wireless and was reminded that agents once recruited should invariably be allotted code names. Kalousis, for instance, was henceforth to be referred to as Blue Eyes. Although I had no experience of cryptography, I wondered even then if I had a secure means of communication. My suspicions were later amply confirmed.

All three of us were fitted out with battledress and Kalousis, who was due to set up shop in Ioannina, was also given some suitable civilian clothing. I carried my bank of a hundred sovereigns in a belt that I wore under my shirt and was instructed (rightly) never to remove it, even in bed. When finally we were shown the list of stores to be packed into the containers to accompany our flight we were told to limit our personal effects to the minimum. I had therefore to argue the case for taking with me what the Greek office considered was a quite unnecessary number of books. Apart from Greek and German dictionaries, my ration was finally limited to Karl Marx's *Capital*, Macaulay's *History of England*, the *Oxford Book of English Verse*, *War and Peace*, *Emma* and *Pride and Prejudice*.

As we flew back to the aerodrome at Tokra in Libya, which was used for all Balkan operations, I felt tense and excited but above all relieved. I reckoned it was mathematically impossible to make two false starts in less than three months. This time I was confident of meeting my primary objective of getting back into the fighting war, and I had a strong premonition, which was proven in the event, that I would have little difficulty in cooperating with SOE – or, as I was training myself to call it, MO4. By the time we had landed in Tokra, Iraq and Yugoslavia seemed to belong to another world.

As a final personal briefing of what Epirus might look like, I remembered Byron and turned to Canto the Second of *Childe Harold's Pilgrimage*, and wondering as the year 1943 was closing, how much would have changed when

> Morn dawns; and with it stern Albania's hills,
> Dark Suli's rocks, and Pindus' inland peak,

Robed half in mist, bedewed with snowy rills,
Arrayed in many a dun and purple streak
Arise; and as the clouds around them break
Disclose the dwelling of the mountaineer:
Here roams the wolf – the eagle whets his beak –
Birds – beasts of prey – and wilder men appear
And gathering storms around convulse the closing year.

Two

On this occasion there was no hitch and we were spared the delay of my earlier experience. A crew of New Zealanders had the plane prepared for us and we took off, shortly after arriving at Tokra, under a full moon during the night of 19 December 1943. It was a long and circuitous flight to Epirus during which we snatched a little sleep. The pilot saw the triangle of fires a long way off, so we were harnessed into our parachutes in ample time. As we circled the target, I remember feeling a sudden sense of calm and release of nervous strain. No power on earth could now get me back to Cairo. That seemed an achievement in itself. The pilot signalled that the next time round he would drop us. The hatch was lifted and we moved into position, all three of us hunched round the circle. The despatcher tapped my shoulder and I swung my legs down, stiffened straight and jumped.

My next reaction was that it had worked. I felt the tug under my armpits, which meant that my parachute was open. I was dropping straight, showing that there was no wind. Moments of extreme exhilaration are rare and unforgettable. This was one of them as I glided down toward a new white world that was suddenly revealed in a mountain landscape of snow, made bright and extraordinarily beautiful by the fullness of the moon. I was also conscious of the stillness all around me after the din of the aircraft, broken only by a light crackle of rifle fire, which I correctly guessed to be a skirmish between EDES and ELAS. I landed in a canopy of powder snow, so softly that it would have done no harm to a newborn baby.

As I was gathering up my parachute, I heard a shout and in a minute I was greeted by Fred Wright, the SOE officer who led the reception party that had been sent to meet us. Soon a chorus of voices announced the safe landing of Kalousis and Katsikakis. We gathered together before Wright led us up the steep hill to the village of Plaisia, our stores having been loaded somewhat indiscriminately onto the backs of mules or old women, who were bent double by the weight. It was an early insight into a new kind of man's world. In the village every house appeared to have a light in it and there was a crowd outside Wright's house to organize our welcome.

The first thing that struck me was the depth of their curiosity, as we were all three submitted to a most friendly but persistent interrogation, which in other circumstances might have taken place in a police station. Kalousis had to interpret my replies and then speak for himself. I was asked: What part of England did I come from? When and where was I born? What did my father do? What was the composition of my family? Was my younger brother also in the Army? Where was he serving? Was he married? Where did we live in London? Was London much bigger than Athens? With these probing questions, some estimate was made of the three new members of their community. I had not expected such instant interest in our arrival, nor the warmth of our reception. Wright was quick to warn me, however, that the same questions were put to everyone who appeared in the village for the first time; they did not therefore indicate either our charm or our importance. He had prepared a meal for us and I had a hip flask of whisky. We sat up till dawn, quite undisturbed that Katsikakis reported that his wireless set had taken a bad landing and one of the containers with the charging engine, battery and spares had not been found. In fact it had been an inefficient drop, as we landed some way off the target; but none of that seemed to matter.

It was from Wright that I began to assemble some of the answers to the many questions I had been asking in Cairo. He described how he had personally witnessed the start of the latest skirmish between ELAS and EDES, which was followed by an unvarnished account of his life during the previous months that reflected his frustration, as a trained saboteur, at having inflicted so little damage on the Germans. All his energies had been concentrated on the political assignment of trying to prevent an extension of the civil war between EDES and ELAS. He had not opted to be a political officer and made no claim to have such qualifications. But his cheerfulness was infectious and I welcomed the instructions he had received to take me over in the next few days to meet Zervas and Tom Barnes at Derviziana, EDES headquarters, which he described as 'about eight hours' from Plaisia, on the other side of the main Ioannina-Arta road. This was my first indication that distance in the mountains was always measured in walking time. We sat talking through the remainder of the night while Kalousis and Katsikakis were given a suitable welcome next door.

The following day, Wright proposed that we should set off to Derviziana as soon as I felt ready to move and cautiously asked me how fit I was. This was a sensible inquiry, but I stupidly replied that I could take anything. In fact I had been given no appropriate training course in Cairo to prepare me to move about in the mountains. He also noticed that the spikes on my boots were different from his and was surprised that I had been dropped in with other different forms of equipment, including a different wireless set. These were small details, but they showed the separation in Cairo between our two organizations.

He prudently suggested that I should spend a day or two finding my feet and keeping in touch with Kalousis and Katsikakis, reporting our safe arrival to the Greek office in Cairo (over his wireless channel because our own could not be mended), and in general becoming acclimatized. Wright shrewdly saw that it would take some time to turn any of us, myself especially, into *andartes*, which was the name covering all guerrillas, in and out of uniform, who belonged to the Greek Resistance.

The delay gave me the chance to hear Wright's account of the Gorgopotamos operation and the part Zervas and Barnes had played in it. He assumed, of course, that I knew what he was talking about, whereas in fact I was learning for the first time what had happened and the effect it had had on the development of both EDES and ELAS. It was also from Wright that I first heard of Myers and Woodhouse, and he added a laudatory account of Zervas's nationalist virtues and Barnes's committed loyalty to him and EDES, which Wright shared unconditionally.

The delay also allowed me to spend Christmas Eve in Plaisia and go to the midnight service in the village church, not a word of which I understood; but it moved me intensely and made me feel part of this strange new life. Early on Christmas morning, Wright and I set off for Derviziana.

We were not long out of Plaisia before he warned me not to walk so fast; he quickly saw that I had everything to learn. After an hour I was puffing like a steam engine, and privately wondering whether my pride or my physical incapacity would predominate. As it was now plain to Wright that he had a beginner on his hands, he called a long halt to explain the simple tactics we would use to cross the Ioannina-Arta road, along which the Germans, knowing the crossing points that were normally used, kept regular patrols. All we had to do was to creep down close to the roadside and watch the pattern of the patrol over a couple of hundred yards. When they had their backs turned to us, we would nip across. It gave me confidence to learn that Wright had done it at least ten times. In fact, it worked out exactly as he had described. The patrol heard the scamper of the mules and fired a few aimless shots, but we were well away and quite safe in a matter of minutes.

A night crossing was rightly reckoned to be child's play and I never heard of anyone being caught. We pushed on fast until the main road was a safe distance away, then rested in a village where a light in the window meant that hospitality would automatically be offered. This, at least, gave a contemporaneous ring to another part of Canto the Second:

> . . . The Suliotes stretched the welcome hand . . .
> And filled the bowl, and trimmed the cheerful lamp
> And spread their fare – though homely, all they had:
> Such conduct bears Philanthropy's rare stamp:
> To rest the weary and to soothe the sad
> Doth lesson happier men, and shames at least the bad.

We had walked through the night and reached Derviziana at dawn. On arrival, Wright looked as if he had had a full night's sleep; in contrast, I was utterly exhausted and ashamed of myself for being so. In this condition I was put straight to bed and collapsed into sleep fully dressed, as soon as I had taken off my boots.

When I had recovered, it was to find myself in a large village with walnut trees and a magnificent view across the valley of Lakka Souli. All around me was the bustle of business in EDES headquarters, orders given in raucous shouts by bearded *andarte*

47

commanders, bandoliers crisscrossed over their battledress. But before I had time to absorb the atmosphere of this brave new world, Wright led me to meet Tom Barnes, a smiling, easygoing New Zealander, who was the senior officer in charge of the Allied Military Mission to EDES. His opening remark was to welcome my presence, and I soon saw why Wright had spoken so warmly of him and had confidently dismissed my earlier fears that he would give me a cool reception. I was relieved to hear him promise full cooperation and say that I should instantly forget we were representing two different organizations in Cairo. It would be a relief, he said, to shift all intelligence responsibilities on to me, and he frankly admitted disinterest in this side of the business and his lack of concern with Zervas's intelligence on the German order of battle. He was clearly on firmer ground, however, when our discussion turned to EAM/ELAS. After much personal reminiscence, beginning with his experience of the Gorgopotamos operation, he spoke as Zervas's mouthpiece and quickly warned me to discard all that I might have heard in Cairo in the latter's disfavour.

I was then taken to see Zervas himself in the simple little village house which served as his headquarters. He welcomed me as Captain Jim, a form of address to which I had not yet become accustomed. Boulis Metaxas – no relation of the dictator – was the interpreter during the talk that followed among the four of us. Barnes explained the purpose of my mission, adding, to my surprise, that Zervas could rely on the fact that I would not hesitate to include ELAS in my brief. At this a smile of satisfaction spread over Zervas's face as he began a lengthy account of his troubles with ELAS and the lack of understanding of his position that prevailed in Cairo.

It was some time before we got round to analysing the German order of battle. When we did so, I naturally began to fire questions about the dispositions of the troops under Lanz's command. There was a marked imprecision in his answers. My first reaction was therefore to see that there was some purpose in my mission. The meeting ended with warm handshakes all around and repeated promises of help and cooperation in every respect. Zervas said that he would warn the EDES Committee in Ioannina to assist Kalousis, who, I had explained, would shortly be entering the town to find out what he could about the activities of the German headquarters in western Greece.

Zervas was an impressive and seductive figure. His vast bulk seemed to envelop the small working desk in front of him on which the papers were hidden by his Old Testament beard. With a forage cap worn jauntily on one side of his huge head and a sparkle in his eyes, he was the picture-book guerrilla. What also struck me were the fierceness of his words and gestures when speaking of ELAS, his good humour, and his confidence in himself and his ultimate victory over all comers. I had been expecting something different, someone less self-assured.

After meeting Zervas, I was taken to see Komninos Pyromaglou, his second-in-command and political adviser, with whom I had a much longer and more educative conversation in French, and hence without an interpreter. Although I had been given no briefing on him, I sensed immediately that Pyromaglou was a completely different kind of person from Zervas. Although his beard and battledress made him look the part of a guerrilla commander, a few minutes' conversation revealed his former academic background and experience of teaching and indoctrinating the uninitiated. Finding me a keen listener and correctly assuming that I had been dropped into Greece, like all my compatriots, with next to no understanding of how resistance had started and virtually no knowledge of its political background, he proceeded to give me his version of the origin and raison d'être of EDES. This took him back a long way, since his account became a vivid piece of autobiography, ornamented by much gesticulation, with frequent allusions to the political path that Zervas had followed, which was not dissimilar from his own. I saw this as an opportunity to give myself a crash course in Greek politics and encouraged him – although in fact he needed little persuasion – to expound at great length and justify the course of action he had taken in his political life. I spent most of the next two days in his company peppering him with questions and greedily acquiring much of the basic information I had tried in vain to obtain in Cairo. In particular, I started to grasp the vital importance of the constitutional issue and the role of the King, and the personality problems that so profoundly divided the Greek political world.

Pyromaglou described how he and Zervas had fought on the side of the Allies in the First World War, and had been followers of Eleftherios Venizelos in his feud with King Constantine over both the desirability, and the likelihood of a German victory. At that stage, Venizelist opposition focused on the person of King Constantine. But the monarchy as an institution had been the supremely divisive issue of Greek politics since at least 1915-16. This division had been even further emphasized in the aftermath of the revolution of 1922, headed by the military leaders Nicholaos Plastiras and Stylianos Gonatas, which followed in the wake of the disastrous Greek defeat in Asia Minor. This led to the abdication of King Constantine, who was succeeded by his son, King George II, and to the convening of a military tribunal which sentenced to death six of King Constantine's leading advisers, including his Prime Minister and Commander-in-Chief. Thereafter, the republican and royalist causes were identified with the Venizelists and anti-Venizelists respectively. The electoral victory of the Venizelists in 1923, and their strong backing from officers of the Army and Navy, resulted in King George's decision to leave Greece at the end of that year without formally abdicating. For the next twelve years Greece was a republic. Both Zervas and Pyromaglou had been followers of General Plastiras since 1922.

The Army had become a political instrument with the formation of the Republican Officers' League under the leadership of General Alexander Othonaios, who had been president of the military tribunal that had court-martialled the six advisers to King Constantine. Among the League's members were Saraphis, a republican officer of distinction (whom ELAS had induced to change sides and become their Commander-in-Chief after they had smashed his own resistance group in March 1943) and Euripides Bakirtzis and Psarros, who were to figure in a later part of Pyromaglou's story when he described the formation of EKKA, the third of the resistance movements. All these officers gained promotion under the first Greek republic at the expense of royalists such as Alexander Papagos, who became Chief of the General Staff in the Metaxas dictatorship in 1936 and was Commander-in-Chief in the Albanian war; Constantine Maniadakis, the Minister under Metaxas who had played the leading role in breaking up the Greek Communist party; and

George Tsolakoglou, who had formed the first Quisling government of occupied Greece after capitulating to the Germans in April 1941. Mention of these names showed how the divisions in the Greek Army stretched back to the twenties. Pyromaglou brushed over the part Zervas had played in supporting the coup d'état in 1925 of General Pangalos, who had assumed command of the Republican Officers' League. But he remained constant in his praise of Plastiras. When the monarchy was restored in 1935, Pyromaglou described King George as 'the leader of the anti-Venizelists'; but this was an almost kind reference to the King's political role when compared with his 'fascist performance', as he called it, of installing a royalist dictatorship under Metaxas on 4 August 1936, which had destroyed all parliamentary political life and led to Pyromaglou's exile in Paris, where he had regained contact with Plastiras. In 1941, acting on Plastiras's orders, he had made his way back to Greece through occupied Europe to contact Zervas and help him form, a year later, what ultimately emerged as the EDES movement. When Zervas began to operate in southern Epirus in the summer of 1942, he could count on no more than a hundred followers. After the successful Gorgopotamos operation in November 1942 their numbers had quickly risen to some five hundred and now, by the end of 1943, he was in command of an organized military force – with the key posts held by regular officers – of over 5,000 men.

It was not, however, on numbers, military objectives or guerrilla tactics that Pyromaglou wished to enlighten me. His mind was exclusively riveted on EDES's political image. Given the political life of Plastiras since 1922, Zervas's consistently anti-royalist past and, above all, the King's personal involvement in Metaxas's coup, how was it possible, Pyromaglou argued, for EDES to have been founded with other than clear republican objectives? This led him to speak of the King with venom, and contrasted sharply with the fact that at my meeting with Zervas the King's name had not been mentioned – probably because Zervas had been speaking in the presence of Barnes, among others. I was, of course, lost when Pyromaglou questioned me about British policy in a clear attempt to see whether I would be the bearer of good tidings in announcing or even hinting that there might be a change in what he called Churchill's adamant support of the King. It was fortunate that he did not press me for answers, as I would have made the worst of first impressions if I had followed my instructions and said that it was not my business to discuss such matters.

After making the point that Tsouderos's government in exile in Cairo now had some claim to legitimacy, because it had rid itself of the worst of Metaxas's followers and was basically Venizelist and republican in composition, Pyromaglou turned at last to the problems of the other resistance movements. On EAM/ELAS, he spoke with a mixture of anger, bitterness and disappointment, hoping that even I had been made aware in Cairo of their proven treachery in initiating the attacks on EDES in October 1943. He assumed – wrongly, of course – that I knew what had happened when the joint *andarte* mission had come to Cairo in the previous August. It was from him that I learned how the representatives of EAM/ELAS, EDES and EKKA had been brought out of Greece by Myers and Wallace. Indeed, it was the first time I had heard of the existence of EKKA (National and Social Liberation) under the leadership of Colonel Psarros and George Kartalis, formerly a Populist but a confirmed anti-royalist since Metaxas's coup, about both of whom Pyromaglou spoke with affection and respect. He described EKKA as an organization parallel to EDES and in no sense less anti-royalist or anti-Communist in its political orientation. It had begun independently of both EDES and EAM and might have had even closer links with EDES if there had not been what he called 'personality problems'. Although he did not say so, I guessed that he was referring to the doubts a person like Kartalis might reasonably be expected to have had about Zervas's political reliability. In any event, EKKA had not taken to the field until March 1943 in the Parnassos area where EAM/ELAS was already operating. Three months later there were clashes. Another observation Pyromaglou made was the unfortunate fact that EKKA's delay in starting armed resistance until 1943 meant that it had lost the opportunity of participating in the Gorgopotamos operation in November 1942. If it had done so, EDES and EKKA might have come together. He stressed that both were still committed to the objective of a united resistance movement, in spite of all their vain attempts to achieve this end, owing to the intransigence of EAM.

Pyromaglou went on to describe his close cooperation with Kartalis while they were members of the joint *andarte* mission in Cairo in August 1943 when, in agreement with the EAM/ELAS representatives, all three resistance movements had stated their claim to seats in Tsouderos's government in exile, and had demanded a statement from the King that he would not return to Greece after the war unless there was a plebiscite in his favour. In fact, nothing happened, since the so-called negotiations with the King, the Greek government in exile, the British Embassy and SOE never got under way, resulting in what he described as a fiasco. Pyromaglou emphasized the loss of this golden opportunity for the British authorities – who held all the cards – to come to terms with the extent and nature of the opposition to the King among such widely different sections of the Greek Resistance.

In his view the prime beneficiary of this failure of the meetings in Cairo had been EAM/ELAS. At the same time he did not conceal his respect for EAM as a political organization and said that a similar revolutionary impetus was needed within EDES to make it compete as the democratic socialist alternative. He thought it was inconceivable that Greece would revert after liberation to the kind of right-wing dictatorship that Metaxas had imposed, or that the main prewar political parties could be revived. Both the Populists and the Liberals were irrevocably discredited, in his opinion, because they had opted out of 'Free Mountain Greece' by steering clear of any formal affiliation with EDES. I was impressed by more than one of his passing remarks that it might still be possible to patch up some kind of a truce between EDES and ELAS in spite of his earlier failures to do so at Liascovo and Pertouli in the summer of 1943.

When our talks – which were mainly monologues from Pyromaglou because of my embarrassing ignorance – finally came to an end, I had good reason to thank him warmly for giving me the kind of briefing I had tried and failed to obtain in Cairo. I could see why Zervas needed a political animal like Pyromaglou and was relieved that he had taken for granted the fact that I should be concerned with the political scene. When we parted, I said for the record, rather tamely, as I had told Zervas, that the purpose of my mission was to report on the German order of battle in western Greece; but my remark happily made no impression on him as he wished me well and encouraged me to keep in contact with him on political developments.

My meeting in Derviziana gave me much to think about as Wright and I began our return to Plaisia. Everyone in SOE had given me a warmer welcome than I had believed likely from the briefings I had been given in Cairo. No one had mentioned the Costa Lawrence affair and I had, as it were, presented my credentials to Zervas. This meant that I could send Kalousis off to Ioannina as soon as I got back. On the whole, I reckoned that I could form no estimate of what my mission was likely to achieve.

On our return I began to acquire the slow *andarte* trudge by following behind Wright. Once again we crossed the road behind the backs of the German patrol which this time did not even notice us, but after an hour or two my whole body began to droop with fatigue. I was both untrained and unfit. My feet had not been hardened, as they should and could so easily have been, by appropriate training in Cairo. I began by brushing aside Wright's suggestion for a rest out of a stupid fear that he would think the better of me if I carried on. But the pretence did not last long and at a certain moment my legs literally collapsed and I fell down in slow motion. It was a humiliating experience. Wright took my boots off and found that both my feet were bleeding. He hoisted me on to a mule where I sat side saddle, hating myself and feeling ashamed. My pride was as wounded as my feet and I knew that when we reached Plaisia, the whole village would be told of my pitiable performance.

This in fact happened, but in an odd way. As we came into the village, there was a shout that I had been wounded and the first inquiry was whether ELAS or the Germans had found me as their target. When Wright explained that neither was the case and that I just was not strong enough to manage a simple night march from Derviziana, the little crowd that had gathered round his house mixed their sympathy with understandable contempt.

On 29 December 1943 I sent my first signal to the Greek office (over Wright's wireless channel as Katsikakis was untrained to repair his own set) reporting my contact with Zervas and Barnes and the former's clearance for Kalousis to enter Ioannina. I added my intention to stay in Plaisia with Wright until ejected by ELAS or the Germans. In the next few days I sent Kalousis into

Ioannina, and Wright put me in touch with three *andartes* from a nearby village who were well placed to report the German road traffic from Ioannina to Preveza.

They were a simple but naturally intelligent group (I code-named them 'Trio'), who responded quickly to my instructions how to describe the vehicle signs on German transport. By this means we could identify their units by referring to my copy of the captured German handbook with which I had been supplied in Cairo. This group later organized their village into keeping a regular watch on every military convoy and sent their reports to me by runner twice a week for the next eight months. The whole village took pride in its work and proved the authenticity of their observation by drawing the vehicle signs with sufficient accuracy for me to be able to make them match with those in the handbook I was holding. The keenest and best of the team was virtually illiterate; but this in no way decreased the value of the intelligence they provided.

It was an early indication of two things: the first was the relative ease of acquiring the military information needed by GHQ in Cairo, and the second was the eagerness of everyone around us to be mobilized into any form of anti-German activity. This meant, as I was soon to discover, that the traditional view of intelligence as an operation carried out by secret agents had virtually no relevance in such circumstances. In villages where everyone knew what everyone else was thinking and doing every hour of every day and night, it would have been a palpable misnomer to have described such informants as secret agents. This, as I later learned, was to give me problems in explaining the reality of the situation to the Greek office in Cairo.

On 4 January 1944 Katsikakis was able to signal our first traffic report (still on Wright's borrowed set) and three days later the EDES Committee in Ioannina, on Zervas's instructions, sent me a long, if confused account of the dispositions of the German 1st Mountain Division. Soon afterward Kalousis returned from Ioannina with much the same information drawn from his initial contact with the EDES Committee, and I saw that our first problem would be to acquire independent sources. Fortunately, Kalousis had made a good start by encountering a retired gendarmerie officer named Kharalambos Varfis, who came from

55

his own village, Himara, in northern Epirus. This, as I soon learned, was the equivalent of a family connection and meant that Varfis immediately joined forces with Kalousis and put at his disposal a wide range of contacts in Ioannina, including one working in the German Town Major's office.

The job had begun with the help and cooperation of Tom Barnes and I felt less of a crock. The novelty of life in the champagne air of a mountain village, the excitement of a new existence, and a fierce determination to prove to myself that I could carry out my tasks: all this gave a bite to life as each new day dawned. It was just as well that what strength I had returned to me, because on 10 January, the Germans sent up a strong patrol, which caused us to make a quick move from Plaisia to Agnanda. I managed the march without difficulty and never thereafter failed to keep up with the others.

It was here that I met another SOE officer, an attractive Irishman named Spike Moran, who introduced himself without a qualm as the person who had shot my predecessor, Costa Lawrence. Moran was a sabotage expert with many months' experience in Epirus and had already earned a reputation for skill at his job, as well as being an instant success with the girls. At the same time, he had learned Greek with unusual speed, acquiring, as he told me, both his vocabulary and his grammar in bed. We became friends from our first encounter and I was grateful to him for saying straightaway that when we got to know one another a little better, he would tell me what happened to Lawrence, and why. In fact, it was my third night in Agnanda, when we had some drink inside us, that he told me the story.

It seemed that soon after Lawrence's arrival doubts arose about his sanity. Whatever he may have felt, it was the act of an imbecile to stride from village to village pouring open scorn on Zervas and at the same time to sing the praises of ELAS. Naturally this performance was reported to Zervas by everyone within earshot. Indeed, he had been thrown out of two villages for such behaviour. The fact that he called himself an American Greek and wore British battledress made him incomprehensible to anyone of any nationality in EDES territory. Since he was formally attached to the Allied Mission, Barnes had to answer to both Myers and Zervas for Lawrence's activities. From the start

Zervas was outraged and Barnes, with much embarrassment, tried to calm him down. But Lawrence's performance went from bad to worse. His case became more serious when it became known to everyone in the town that two of his so-called agents in Ioannina were in the pay of the Germans.

It was then that Barnes told Moran to keep a protective watch on Lawrence without, if possible, raising his suspicions. They lived in the same village for a while, during which time Moran became increasingly sure that Lawrence was playing tricks; but it was only when the Germans began to picket the area more closely that he became convinced. One evening Lawrence suggested that they should make a joint reconnaissance of the German positions. Moran agreed and they set out together. After a short distance Lawrence said he felt tired and sat down for a rest. Moran continued on his way and then turned round to watch what Lawrence was doing. When he saw him flashing his torch across the valley and receiving recognition signals from the village which the Germans were occupying, he realized that the plain purpose of the reconaissance was to betray him. He sauntered back to Lawrence and asked him casually to whom he had been signalling. Lawrence became flustered and denied that he had been using his torch. Moran then shot him dead.

The story was told with such calm and assurance that I found it hard to disbelieve; but I did not report it until a month later, in February 1944 when much of the circumstantial detail had been confirmed by other SOE officers, notably Tom Barnes. Later in the year when I went to Athens to wind up my mission, the head of the Greek office refused to reveal to me how and why Lawrence had been recruited. In answer to my report in February he merely signalled that my version of what happened did not square with what he had been told at the time by SOE in Cairo. In any event, I should not 'waste too much time or juice on the matter'.

I followed these instructions but could not help acquiring further embarrassing information. First, I learned that the name Costa Lawrence was certainly a pseudonym, but it was only part of his cover story that he was an American Greek. In fact he was from Corinth and he had served as a wireless operator on a number of British ships, which probably explained how the head of the Greek office in Cairo had known him in Patras before the war. I also discovered that he had been dropped in Greece at the end of 1942 as wireless operator to Captain Agathoklis Constantinides, who soon abandoned his intelligence mission to form an *andarte* unit within the EDES organization. In this way, Costa Lawrence found himself on his own. It was, however, the postwar published evidence portraying Costa Lawrence as a martyr in the EAM/ELAS cause that more than confirmed the gist of what I had heard about him (though the circumstances were different) and explained the reticence of the Greek office in their attempts to brush the whole matter under the rug and cover up a palpably egregious error in recruiting such a person.

Saraphis's account, published in Athens in 1946,[7] gives a different version of the circumstances in which Lawrence was shot, but in all other respects amply substantiates the claim that he was an EAM/ELAS propagandist. Saraphis wrote:

In Epirus there was a Greek officer working as a secret agent of the British Intelligence Service under the name of Kosta Lawrence. He was equipped with his own radio and transmitted his reports directly to Cairo. We knew nothing of him, but he was accused by the British themselves of helping the Germans and betraying the guerrillas' positions. Brigadier Eddie [Myers] asked us to arrest him and we gave the necessary instructions to the 8th Division. Aris [Velouchiotis] who was in Epirus with Zervas at this time, personally gave verbal instructions that a special detachment be formed to make the arrest. The detachment duly arrested Lawrence, handed him over to another British officer, Lieutenant S [Spike Moran] and then set out with the two men for the British Mission. Eddie [Myers] received the news of the arrest with great delight. During the journey, Lieutenant S [Spike Moran] shot Lawrence claiming that he had tried to escape. The murder was committed to prevent the truth coming out. However, Lawrence's diary fell into ELAS's hands and was sent to headquarters in whose archives it is today. It is a hard-backed exercise book written mainly in English, though in some places in Greek with Latin characters. As no one else at headquarters knew English, I read it myself and was thunderstruck at what I read. As well as information about the enemy, Lawrence had been sending Cairo political reports concerning the situation in Epirus, the various organizations, the strengths of EAM and EDES, the morale of the people, their democratic sentiments, their sympathy with ELAS and their dislike of EDES. Moreover, he condemned various arbitrary

[7] English translation published as *ELAS: Greek Resistance Army* (Merlin Press, 1980). See pp.176-7.

actions of Brigadier Eddie [Myers] who had tried to deprive him of his radio. Inserted betwen the pages of the diary was a letter he had written to Eddie accusing him of serving City interests. He was completely sincere and objective. Also inserted in the diary was a telegram from the Cairo Secret Service reminding him that he had sworn allegiance and undertaken certain obligations, and warning him that if he did not carry them out, action would be taken against him. The upshot was that he was murdered for speaking the truth and not sending reports which accorded with the wishes and desires of his Service. Unfortunately ELAS abetted his murder by arresting him, not realizing that it was acting against a sincere man and a friend. Had we known, we could have protected him.

A much later account in a book called *Laurels and Tears*, published in Athens in 1981 (but not translated into English), by Christos Kainourgios, a former ELAS officer, gives a different setting to the shooting of Lawrence by an unnamed British officer, but in other respects it substantiates the claim that he was ideologically committed to ELAS, citing as evidence the fact that Lawrence had handed over two wireless sets to an ELAS commander to emphasize his disgust with the British Mission for supplying EDES but not ELAS with arms and ammunition. In this version (on page 164), he was credited with blurting out that 'the British were fascists' and his superiors in Cairo were 'faithful servants and agents of British imperialism'.

Strangely enough, Spike Moran, who had shot my predecessor, took it upon himself to help me in every possible way. When I told him of my objectives, he quickly saw that I needed a strategically well-placed base from which to operate. Opening a map, he explained to me with impressive detail the pros and cons of a number of villages of which he had personal experience. Finally, he recommended one called Tseritsana on the other side of the main Ioannina-Arta road where he had friends to whom he would introduce me. He correctly judged that it was in a good position for my purposes: seven hours by foot from Ioannina, which was my main target, and three hours from Zervas's headquarters and the Allied Military Mission at Derviziana, with both of which I would necessarily need to be in regular contact. I readily accepted his advice, most of all because I sensed the advantage of being introduced by Moran and thereby establishing precisely the opposite reputation from that of my predecessor.

So when the German patrols left Agnanda, we moved to Tseritsana by easy stages and arrived on 14 January 1944.

Although I had been in Epirus for less than a month, I had seen enough of the country to realize that it was ideally suited for guerrilla operations. All movement was by mule tracks: there were no roads through the long valleys where isolated villages were cut into the sides of the hills. In this beautiful wilderness of mountain gorges and crevices, every yard of every footpath was known to the *andartes* of each locality. I quickly saw that their geographical expertise, which was constantly at our disposal, was something that could never be acquired by the Germans. It meant that in any game of hide and seek, the laugh would always be on the seeker. I also sensed from all the British officers I had met their unconditional reliance on everyone around us. Indeed, not one instance of treachery, apart from the Lawrence episode, had ever been reported. The political geography of the area was no less well known. A village where ELAS had sympathizers would be described with exact details of precisely whom to avoid and why, and how this should be carried out. To be operating in these surroundings brought a sense of confidence and security and a realization of the political and military advantages that were on our side.

By the same token, Lieutenant General Hubert Lanz was beset with severe problems. Little did any of us know that this highly educated officer with a good knowledge of classical Greece had an unusually sensitive understanding of the political geography of the area under his command. He was not at all the normal German general we all assumed him to be. This was later revealed in his analysis of partisan warfare in the mountains (which he wrote in 1950 while he was in Landsberg prison after his trial before the United States Military Tribunal at Nuremberg in 1947), based on the experience of his command of north-western Greece and southern Albania in 1943 and 1944. From the Nuremberg tribunal, a clear picture had earlier emerged of Lanz's character and military career from the extensive evidence of a wide variety of officers and other ranks who had served with him in Russia and Greece. In fact, his appointment to the command of the XXII Mountain Corps in Ioannina, which was a secondary theatre of operations, amounted to demotion. He had spent most of the first two years of the Russian campaign in the thick of the fighting and had been decorated for his services. But at the same time his strict Catholic upbringing and his refusal to join the Nazi party had provided some politically damaging evidence against him. He insisted, for instance, that captured Soviet commissars should not be shot unless they were engaged in military combat; this contravened a personal order of the Führer. In the spring of 1943 Lanz had been summoned by General Schmundt, Chief of the Army Personnel Office, and told that his promotion and assignment to a main theatre of operations depended on him severing his close public connections with the Catholic Church and binding himself to the Nazi Party. Lanz refused on both scores. His refusal landed him in Greece.

At the start of his own account[8], Lanz justifiably drew attention 'with the eyes of a soldier' to all the conditions in the area under his command that favoured partisan warfare.

This was a wild, thinly populated, mountainous country which winds through lonely, narrow passes. For miles there are only woods, rocks and loneliness. There lie the notorious Grammos mountains. From here to the south, the Pindus region extends like a gigantic stone barrier, a rugged, romantic mountainous country with innumerable peaks and rocky summits rising to more than 6,500 feet. Only one single line of communication cuts this long, drawn-out mountain range from east to west, the road from Trikalla over the 5,500 feet high Metsovo pass to Ioannina, the capital of Epirus. In the summer of 1943, when the German occupation troops came out of Albania into Epirus, the partisans held this road denying its use to the Germans.

All of southern Albania and the north-western part of Epirus is one mass of mountains with many high and almost inaccessible mountain ranges through which only narrow paths lead. Pitiful mountain villages nestle here and there on the steep slopes.

Stone huts cling to the cliffs. These are the settlements of the mountain peasants. Between the Pindus and the Adriatic, an area approximately ninety miles wide, numerous additional mountain ranges extend from north to south in whose loneliness lie isolated villages connected with each other by poor roads. The only larger locality is Paramithia, situated on the western slopes of a mighty rock massif, which played an

[8] Ms.P-055a: 'Partisan Warfare in the Mountains (Based upon Experience in Greece and Southern Albania 1943-4)'. Historical Division European Command. Translators: Franke/Luetzkendorf.

important part in partisan battles (during the end of the German occupation). The road from Ioannina to the small port of Igoumenitsa, the German supply base for the island of Corfu, led through the partisan area of Paramithia. Approximately fifty miles to the south, at the edge of extensive olive groves, lies the port of Preveza. The remaining settlements on the rocky coast are small smugglers' lairs which, in their concealed location, served as secret transfer points for the supply of the partisans by sea.

The Gulf of Arts (where the naval battle of Actium took place in 30 B.C.) gives the landscape its peculiar character. The vast expanse of water with its innumerable inlets and bays, provided an ideal hiding place for partisan bands. In the east, the Gulf of Arta meets the mountains along the underbrush lined edge of which the only north-south road passes over an artificial causeway, constructed between the water and the cliffs without any possibility of deviation. Thus this lone communication line between Ioannina in the north and Agrinion in the south is an easy prey for partisans and a trap for all who are dependent upon the road.

To the south of the great gulf, the scenery is again dominated by chains of hills between which lie lakes and swamps; here also wide and lonely stretches again provide good refuge for the partisans. Until the Metsovo road was reopened all supplies for the German forces in Epirus moved on the north-south road. This extended from the end of the railway line at Florina through a pass 5,200 feet high and thence by another pass through the spurs of the Grammos mountains to the Greek border south of Leskovits. There it passed over two emergency bridges in order to reach headquarters at Ioannina, after covering a road distance of approximately 170 miles. Here was the distribution and relay point.

Constantly watched by the partisans and their numerous accomplices in the city, and reported in advance to the bands in the country outside, the columns with their valuable cargoes of food, ammunition and fuel, moved in guarded convoys to the coastal supply base at Igoumenitsa or the southern division of Agrinion, each time again crossing 60 to 120 miles of guerrilla infested mountainous country . . . The fact that no adequate security service could be established on these vital roads naturally facilitated the activity of the partisans. The numerous construction works on these mountainous roads seemed made for acts of sabotage by the guerrillas. Every demolition of one of these objects brought traffic to a standstill for hours, even days. During the entire period of the occupation hardly a night, and from the summer of 1944 not a single day passed without a surprise attack, a mine explosion or another act of sabotage on one of the supply roads . . . A stranger became lost in this stony desert; it was difficult to get one's bearings and impossible to travel without a map or compass.

Moran and I needed neither a map nor a compass in our move from Agnanda to Tseritsana. There Moran introduced me to Major Paul Bathgate, a cheerful SOE officer considerably older than myself, and his French and German-speaking interpreter, Mario Maniakis, a lieutenant in the regular Greek Army aged twenty-five, who told me that he had left his home on the island of Levkas at the end of 1942 and joined EDES in March 1943. After being wounded fighting a German patrol, he had joined the Allied Mission in August 1943 as Bathgate's interpreter. I could sense straightaway that they both had affection and respect for Moran and I could not therefore have been better sponsored. It took me no time to see that behind Maniakis's laughter and happy nature lay exceptional ability, energy and poise – he subsequently reached the rank of lieutenant general – and we quickly became friends.

He and Bathgate agreed that the best place for me to stay in the village was in Nikos's house. He had the advantage of owning three strong mules. If I was to set up a mission of my own, it was explained to me that I would need a reliable mule driver with my own independent transport system. A further recommendation was that Nikos worked closely with Aristides, who was known to be a particularly reliable messenger, having carried out a number of missions for Bathgate. But first, of course, I would have to come to terms with both of them so that our relationship could start on a firm commercial footing.

On the evening of my arrival in mid January, Nikos was summoned by Bathgate. It was explained that I was the last British officer to have been dropped into Epirus and that, if all went well, I would stay in Tseritsana and use it as my base. In order to inflate my importance, Moran said that Zervas had already formed a high opinion of me and that I would be keeping close contact with EDES headquarters, which would involve regular trips to Derviziana with Nikos's mules. He spoke of me as an old friend of long standing, fully deserving of everyone's trust. Soon, he said, the whole village would welcome the day that I came to live with them. It was a fulsome introduction that took me somewhat by surprise. Perhaps it was a bit overdone, because I saw no sign on Nikos's face that he was impressed by this parade of my virtues. At the end of it all, he looked me straight in the eye and remarked that he took for granted all that had been said about me; he would willingly prepare a room for me in his house where I could have the best bed and his wife would ensure that I was properly looked after, but – there was a pause – did I realize that his were the best mules in the whole of Lakka Souli? If I was to set up on my own, I should buy them from him there and then. His price was eight sovereigns each. Time would show that I was on to a bargain. When his words reached me via Maniakis's interpretation, I counted out twenty-four sovereigns and a very firm handshake clinched our partnership for the next nine months. The scene was witnessed by Aristides who gave me his assurance that in his safe hand my messages would be faithfully delivered to any person I chose throughout the valley of Lakka Souli. There were further handshakes, as if an important international treaty had been signed, toasts were exchanged in tsipouro (a strong spirit like raki, which I had drunk in Egypt), laughter and gaiety gripped us all, and I felt relaxed and happy that I had begun to be accepted as a member of their community.

The following day I had what turned out to be a stroke of professional luck. Three students from Ioannina, all under twenty years old, who worked as a team and had done a number of odd jobs for EDES in the past, turned up in the village. Moran knew them well and suggested that I should give them a trial intelligence brief to see how they responded. Using Maniakis as my interpreter, who also recommended them warmly, I was introduced to Leon Tsombos, Vassilis Derekas and Constantinos Economou. I gave them a careful description of what GHQ in Cairo needed to know about the identification of the units under command of XXII Mountain Corps in Ioannina, the names of the commanding officers, the strength and equipment of the tank and artillery regiments, their state of morale, and the organization of Lanz's headquarters. In fact, I fed them morsels and did not serve up the whole meal at our first encounter. I was immediately struck, however, by their alertness and their wish to learn how to report professionally. All three commented on the indifference that Zervas's headquarters had shown hitherto to their offers to work against the Germans. A week later they were back in Tseritsana with a string of identifications, willingly supplied by one of the Greek interpreters on Lanz's staff. They also handed over photographs of German tanks and artillery. This established their credentials as agents and they were code-named 'Cherub'.

Such a quick start surprised me. It also surprised the Greek office in Cairo that the SOE mission had cooperated so readily to put me in business. Indeed, it was the most comforting of discoveries to find no reflection in the field of the interdepartmental problems I had witnessed in Cairo before I set out. By the end of January 1944 I was able to signal a regular series of military reports on the 104th Light Infantry Division in Agrinion and the road traffic between Ioannina, Arta and Preveza, which were buttressed by interrogations of three deserters to EDES from the 1st Mountain Division. For this, Paul Bathgate lent me the services of Mario Maniakis and I soon saw how useful he would be to me. All three deserters were Austrians from a unit in which they reckoned eighty per cent of the other ranks were their compatriots, but all the officers and senior NCOs were German. They willingly handed over their paybooks and answered every question we put to them, showing evident delight that this was a way of taking vengeance on the Germans for whom they expressed undisguised loathing.

It was therefore another stroke of luck when Bathgate was transferred in early February 1944 to the Allied Mission to ELAS in Thessaly. There could be no question of Maniakis, who was an EDES officer, going with him. Bathgate and Maniakis therefore both suggested to me, after clearing the proposal with Zervas and Barnes, that Maniakis should stay in Tseritsana and join my mission. I had no difficulty in securing the approval of the Greek office to his recruitment at five sovereigns a month, and in less than a month I felt I had established myself.

When Bathgate left, Maniakis and I set up shop on the ground floor of a little stone house high on the slope of a hill overlooking the church and the fountain famous throughout the valley of Lakka Souli for its clear spring water. The house belonged to the head man of the village, Costakis Poulias, who carried the grandiose title of 'President of the Community'. But everyone knew him as Costakis. He occupied the floor above us with his wife and two children, Aphrodite and Achilleas. I soon became an adopted member of the family and in this way I was quickly absorbed into the life of the village. Costakis was the centre of administrative authority. All disputes were referred to him and his judgments were considered final. The stream of callers at his door led to Maniakis and myself becoming involved in what amounted to local government, since it was Costakis's habit to spend much of every day discussing with us the problems of the village: the management of the school, the upkeep of the church, the sale of land and personal property and, above all, the settlement of individual wrangles between and, often even within, families.

It was a luxurious life by mountain standards. Costakis kept chickens and goats and in return for the princely rent of three sovereigns a month I was amply supplied with eggs and cheese. In addition, our contacts in Ioannina could bring us good black market food, which was mostly of German origin. I was properly clad for the winter, with more than enough to eat, and sufficient blankets to keep me warm. But just as I was congratulating myself on my good fortune, I suddenly fell ill with what I knew was an attack of walking jaundice. Although I did not turn yellow, my stomach could absorb nothing, and even without a thermometer it was obvious that I had a high temperature. I lay in bed, once again feeling ashamed of myself and wondering what would happen if we had to make a quick move. But providence was on my side, because heavy snow over the whole of Epirus put a stop to much of the three-cornered war between EDES, ELAS and the Germans. When the thaw came, I was on the mend and fortified by German medicine brought to me from Ioannina by Leon Tsombos. By the end of February I was on my feet again and recovering rapidly in the mountain air.

It was at this time that I signalled my first statement showing what I had spent since my arrival. The itemized account (in sovereigns) read as follows: '3 mules, 24; forage for mules, 5; house rent, 3; personal living expenses only 5 because we have been living on much tinned food we brought with us and "golden" exchange value of silk parachute panels. Agents' expenses were Trio 6, Cherub 10, Blue Eyes and his sundry contacts 19. Total 72.' This left me with a running balance of only twenty-eight sovereigns and I put in a strong plea for another drop to be organized as soon as possible with a further seventy sovereigns, as well as a replacement for the charging engine, spare batteries and spare parts that had been lost in the original drop in December. This had meant that I was dependent upon the cooperation of SOE for my wireless communications, *inter permulta alia*, since Katsikakis's lack of training meant that we were continuously asking for their technical help, whenever our wireless set broke down. When I pointed all this out in a stiffly worded signal, I received the comforting reply that a further seventy sovereigns and thirty-six Napoleons (five sovereigns equalled approximately six Napoleons) would be included in my next drop, to which was added the pointless comment that 'the technical side of our work as well as the organization must repeat must be kept absolutely apart from SOE'. This was neither the first nor the last proof that my exchanges with the Greek office were a dialogue of the deaf.

In the first week of March 1944, on one of my visits to Zervas's headquarters, I was given an extensive briefing by Barnes on the armistice agreement that had been signed at the Plaka Bridge in Epirus on 29 February by Saraphis for EAM/ELAS, Pyromaglou for EDES and Psarros and Kartalis for EKKA. Ostensibly, this brought to an end the 'First Round' of civil war between ELAS and EDES and committed all the resistance movements to form a Joint Military Committee and cooperate closely in Allied operations leading up to the liberation of Greece. Barnes expressed his admiration for Woodhouse for having organized the meeting and arranged the agreement, but he did not think it would stick and he said he had warned Zervas not to be misled by Pyromaglou's optimism. After speaking to Barnes, I saw Pyromaglou myself and discovered that he was, in fact, notably cautious about the likely turn of events and certainly did not believe that anything more than a temporary truce had been achieved. This was one of my first indications that Barnes could misinterpret what Pyromaglou said.

While I had been ill, Maniakis and I were able to keep our small organization going and to expand it. Kalousis, who, happily, was a friend of Maniakis, organized a traffic watch on the Ioannina-Metsovo-Trikala road and accurately reported the vehicle signs on the German convoys. He also began to construct a network of his own informants, independent of the EDES organization in Ioannina. Tsombos and his friends (Cherub) quickly discovered that the smallest bribe was enough to induce any of the Italians remaining in Ioannina to betray their German masters. He also co-opted the services of an attractive girl called Loukia Polimenou, whose father was in the police in Corfu and was consequently well placed to identify the German units on the island and report on their movements. Maniakis himself sent an intermediary to contact his brother in Levkas, which meant that we soon had the German positions on the coast in Preveza and Parga closely and regularly covered. He, too, spoke fluent German, which made him one of the few Greeks on the island with whom German officers could relax at the end of the day. Intelligence consequently reached him without his having to search for it. One long report of special interest to GHQ in Cairo gave a detailed description of the dangerously low morale of the troops in the Preveza area where hushed anti-Hitler talk had begun to spread among the other ranks. This had led certain selected officers to wear civilian clothes in the evenings and mix with the men of units they were not directly commanding, in order to gain firsthand knowledge of the growing subversion, and arrest the main culprits. In addition, Maniakis, who showed from the start that he had a flair for intelligence, personally co-opted the services of two regular army officers who were serving in EDES, Captains Zotos and Papadatos. With their help, road traffic controls were established by the Zikos family, who owned a small coffee-house at the Zita bridge on the Arta-Philipeas-Ioannina road, and at the Tiria Bridge on the Ioannina-Igoumenitsa road. From Preveza we also received regular, accurate reports on military movements and identifications from Nikolaos Monasteriotis, a civil engineer employed by the Germans in the public administration, who was a close friend of Maniakis.

When the separate pieces of the jigsaw were put together, a picture of the German order of battle in western Greece began to emerge. As each item of information reached us, it was signalled to the Greek office, which relayed it to GHQ in Cairo. It gave a boost to our morale when appreciative comments were received from GHQ, which, in turn, sent us more and increasingly detailed questionnaires.

Meantime, the whole village not only quickly got to know in some detail what we were doing, but assumed the right to participate in our work. This was scarcely the normal environment of an intelligence bureau and it was something I knew the Greek office would not easily understand. If, however, I had tried to transplant the normal rules of covert activity into these surroundings and had done my best to isolate myself from all those around me, I saw for a start that it would have been impossible. But more importantly, it would have engendered every kind of suspicion that I was working in some way against their interests. It was not difficult to grasp the first fact of life in a mountain village: that if I wanted to stay there and use it as my base, I must abide by its rules and adapt myself to the villagers' way of life. If I did so, their cooperation would be unlimited.

It came as no surprise that each new arrival in Tseritsana, whether he came from a village nearby or from one of the towns in Epirus, was immediately identified and very closely interrogated. Every item of news in his head, true or false, trivial or significant, was quickly extracted, commented upon and instantly relayed to everyone within earshot. But the first person to be informed of every new event was Costakis, the President of the Community. As I lived in his house, all his news quickly became mine. I would be told that Andreas had just been conscripted by the Germans into a labour force for building an airstrip; that Evangelos had a cousin whose brother-in-law was now serving in ELAS against his will and wanted to defect to Zervas; that Marcos's uncle in Ioannina had heard that the Germans would definitely be out of Greece before the summer; that Leftheris had heard from his sister in Arta that EDES was planning an attack on the town in the following week, and that the Germans were so scared by the prospect that they had asked Athens for reinforcements.

I always listened patiently to everything that was told me and naturally assured Costakis and others who approached me directly that every scrap of information was of great value. This was the only deception I practised and it helped me to be accepted as someone they could trust as a member of their community. Hence they found nothing strange in my contact with those who were in fact providing the information I had been sent in to acquire. After Maniakis and I had debriefed our genuine agents, Nikos and Aristides, who were our mule drivers, and Spiro, who cooked for us, would always be waiting outside to ask how the meeting had gone. Was Captain Jim satisfied with your work? Did Mr Mario put questions of his own? Have they asked you to carry out any dangerous assignments? Did you bring news of German plans to attack us? Do they think they are winning? Did Captain Jim say when the British would come to liberate us? What does he think of ELAS? Does he admire Zervas? This volley of questions was regularly fired; I had only to walk through the village after our visitors had gone to be told that Mario's brother was clearly doing a fine job; that Kalousis had a splendid reputation in Ioannina and was giving his soul to his work: which explained perhaps why he had grown thinner in the face and needed to take things easy for a bit; that Tsombos and his group had more cunning than most and could be relied upon to outwit the Germans. All our informers knew very well what could and what could not be revealed about their work to inquisitive questioners. They needed no sermonizing from me or Maniakis to be tight-lipped about how their information was gathered. If indeed they had been indiscreet about the means they used for obtaining their information, I would very soon have heard about it: being told in all innocence how comforting it was to have informers in Lanz's headquarters. But no such indications came to my notice.

Twice a week we sent runners to Zervas in Derviziana with copies of the information we were signalling to Cairo. In this way my position became firmly established with Barnes and Zervas, and I both felt and in fact became an integral part of the SOE mission, which helped me with advances of funds, the maintenace of our wireless communications, and even made no complaint when my first request for supplies was sent to Zervas's dropping ground at Derviziana instead of to Tseritsana. This made even more unreal the repeated instruction from the Greek office that every aspect of my mission should be kept absolutely apart from SOE.

Throughout March we kept up an almost daily flow of information on the German order of battle, which became progressively easier to obtain from Ioannina, Preveza, Arta,

Agrinion, Levkas and Corfu. Maniakis and I spent a sizeable amount of our time interrogating a thin trickle of deserters to EDES, often Austrians, and prisoners from EDES operations on the main Ioannina-Arta road, who handed over their paybooks and readily revealed to us every fact of military intelligence in their disillusioned heads. Both Zervas and Barnes continued to assure me that they welcomed shifting their intelligence responsibilities to my mission. This showed, of course, that their cooperation with my mission was as much rooted in interest as in goodwill. Spared of an additional encumbrance, they had more time to concentrate on what they rightly considered to be their main task. The result of this concatenation of circumstances was that I was surprised, and GHQ in Cairo even more so, that by the end of March a fairly complete picture had been built up. If, as had been anticipated earlier in 1944, there had been an Allied landing, its commander would have known in some detail the strengths, locations and battle experience of his opposition in all the main towns of Epirus. It gave us great pleasure when I was able to relay to our informants the thanks and congratulations of GHQ for the information they had been receiving.

We could follow in detail all the German traffic movements on the main road from Ioannina leading south through Arta and Agrinion. The east-west link from Trikala through the Metsovo pass to Ioannina, and from Ioannina to Igoumenitsa, the German supply base opposite Corfu, were equally well covered. In Ioannina, both Kalousis and Tsombos had set up information networks that were independent of one another. Neither depended on the EDES Committee, whose reports were regularly forwarded to me from Derviziana on Zervas's instructions. Maniakis and I therefore had a means of checking that we were not receiving the same information from three ostensibly different channels.

We could also begin to gauge the scope of Lanz's problem. With the 1st Mountain Division based in Ioannina and the 104th Light Infantry Division in Agrinion, untrained for mountain warfare and short of motor transport, plus some low-grade ancillaries, XXII Mountain Corps had the formidable assignment of protecting the coast against a possible Allied invasion from Himara in Albania to the Gulf of Patras. In addition to his responsibility for a coastline of over 400 miles, Lanz had to ensure the security of an area of about 18,000 square miles against organized resistance movements in southern Albania, Epirus and part of Thessaly. We could see that he was in no position to carry out all his security assignments. He could hold the towns for the good reason that neither EDES nor ELAS were geared to capture them. With difficulty, he could keep his lines of communication open. But he could not realistically plan to destroy either EDES or ELAS in the area under his control. If the towns were his, the mountains were ours.

According to Lanz, in north-western Greece

the partisans concentrated their efforts on the supply roads and the traffic moving along them. They used two types of sabotage: dynamiting and mining. The many artificial constructions along the roads encouraged dynamiting. If a bridge was blown up, traffic was interrupted for several days. Good protection against such sabotage was never found; indeed there were too many of them to protect them all. The draining systems of the bridges were frequently used during the dry season to plant dynamite charges. These were well placed and well camouflaged and they could scarcely be noticed. The manpower problem in this case, as in many others, was of decisive importance. Security detachments and patrols were constantly subjected to surprise attacks with the result that they lost both their personnel and their equipment. It was frequently impossible to give security detachments the necessary strength, as enough troops were not available.

Much worse was the sabotage by well-planted mines which the motorized road patrols were unable to prevent. Especially effective were the 'rock mines' that resembled stones or rocks strewn across the road, which the mine detectors could not locate. The only solution was regularly to clean the main roads of all rocks larger than the size of a man's fist. This was a hazardous operation and it claimed a great many lives.

The gathering of information for the partisans was handled in various ways. In billets, for instance, by stealing, copying or photographing maps, plans and other data. Although the population knew that severe punishment was prescribed for acts of sabotage and espionage, numerous cases occured, in very few of which were culprits actually caught. Losses were seldom reported for fear that the loser would be called to account for his negligence. Whenever the loss was finally known, it was usually too late to apply counter measures. It was impossible to segregate the troops from the population and the population from the partisans.

Even in the towns, as Lanz admitted, the German forces were only in control of the surface of events. 'There was hardly a case', he wrote,

where the partisans were taken completely by surprise. No matter how secretly operations were prepared, they soon had knowledge of them – a feat to us of seeming impossibility. The solution of the riddle lay in their excellently organized communications service. The partisans had their liaison men and spies in almost every part of the population. A single, carelessly spoken word sufficed to inform the guerrillas. Their espionage and communications service functioned perfectly. Such messages were carried over great distances to the partisan camps in a surprisingly short time by peasants familiar with every road and path. Disguised as innocent civilians and peaceful citizens, some kept watch over road traffic day and night from suitable points, while others observed the activities of the occupation troops in their headquarters and bases.

Every town and village was inconspicuously and unceasingly watched. No vehicle arrived or departed without being noted. The population on whom the troops were quartered had constant contact with the occupation forces and through this channel they learned far too much. This information went into the mountains and the many attempts to eliminate the partisans contacts were unsuccessful. The Germans were fully aware of their danger but were quite unable to do anything about it.

The good intelligence we were receiving was a reflection of the skill and determination of our agents. They had the advantage, however, that almost everyone believed that the Germans would soon be gone. In these circumstances open opportunities were offered to our agents to approach those who wished to hedge their bets. This applied particularly to the Germans' local agents, whose identity was common knowledge. Both Kalousis and Tsombos sent me reports on Major Franz Bassamer, in charge of the Sicherheitsdienst (Security Service) in Ioannina, who had control of the Greek civil police, which was, in turn, effectively infiltrated by EDES agents at all levels. His two principal contact men in the town, Feldwebel Hans Enderler and Feldwebel Florian Kusch, were a fat, lascivious pair. Both of them spoke Greek and operated quite openly in the town, employing a retinue of Turks and Romano-Vlachs, whom they innocently considered to be more reliable informers than the Greeks. Their main job was to supply Bassamer with the ritual lists of EAM/ELAS and EDES 'sympathizers'. It required no great skill to find out what they were doing and I quickly warned our own agents not to waste time reporting their tittle-tattle. The interpreters working for the competing intelligence services run by the Abwehr (military intelligence) and the Sicherheitsdienst were, of course, serious targets and it was on them that our main counter-espionage effort was directed. At this stage of the war, such people knew that they had backed the losing side. In the first three months of 1944, when the Allied armies were on the road to Rome, when daylight air superiority over Germany had resulted in the RAF and the U.S. Eighth Air Force bombing German targets 'round the clock' and with the Soviet armies on the borders of Rumania, it was common knowledge that the chances of a German evacuation of the Balkans had greatly increased. Those who were working for the Germans were understandably anxious to take out the best insurance policy available against the day when they would be abandoned by their temporary German masters. Full advantage was taken of this situation, which allowed our agents independently to buy, at the low cost of a handful of sovereigns per man per month, direct knowledge of German intelligence operations. Particularly valuable was the cooperation of Lanz's chief interpreter, who had been educated in Germany before the war. He responded easily to the simple suggestion that no great risk would be involved if he ran off an extra typed copy of the documents he was keeping in his files.

Ioannina was a very small world where everyone knew everyone else. Consequently, you did not have to scout about for long before finding the suitable intermediary who could arrange access to your target. Thereafter, following the ritual haggle over the price, a deal could quickly be clinched by 'payment on results', plus the assurance, 'in the name of the British' (which always sounded impressive), that switching sides could lead to atonement for collaboration with the Germans.

If, however, we had good reason to be satisfied with our coverage of the German forces in the towns, Lanz could be equally certain that our movements and plans in the mountains were no less well known to him. It was not until the eve of the German retreat in October 1944 that I had solid confirmation that our codes – my own, certainly, and SOE's in all likelihood, since they were based on the same system – had been cracked by Lanz's special communications intelligence service. But even as early as March of that year I had begun to suspect that our pride in our knowledge of what the Germans were doing might well be matched in some degree by their knowledge of our activities.

What first raised my suspicions was the evidence we began to collect from Greek agents of the Sicherheitsdienst in Ioannina showing an uncomfortably accurate assessment of EDES's strength and disposition in Epirus, as well as a knowledge of the movements of British officers. When these agents began to divulge the instructions they were receiving and the targets at which they were supposed to aim, there were hints, which I was slow to seize upon at the time, that Lanz was hoping to make Zervas his partner against ELAS. I did not then know, as Lanz was later to reveal in his memoir of 'Partisan Warfare in the Mountains', that his monitors

intercepted partisan radio traffic and could tell with whom they were dealing through the type of technique used. Texts en clair frequently transmitted on the partisan radio with no intention of deception, furnished valuable hints as to the enemy's set up and indicated that their radio training programme had not kept pace with unit strength which greatly increased after the beginning of 1944. Furthermore, it was frequently possible to monitor the guerrillas' radio communication by means of a captured code. In this matter, valuable information or confirmation was obtained. A special radio direction finding service was organized which enabled us to check the enemy's movements by constantly tuning in on the partisan's radio stations. Even the tapping of the guerrilla telephone lines, relatively few though they were, brought some interesting results.

If Lanz was referring in this context to both ELAS and EDES, his account made it plain that he had started negotiating with Zervas at the end of 1943 and was confident by April 1944 that he had come to some form of agreement with him whereby ELAS should be treated as their common enemy. This was certainly not known to me at the time. Nor did I have any inkling until August 1944 that Lanz had some reason to count on what he construed as Zervas's 'loyal attitude'. Indeed, his subsequent allegations of a truce between Zervas and the Germans from February to July 1944 did not square with the fact that Zervas was conducting sporadic operations against the Germans over this period, which resulted in the capture of prisoners whom Maniakis and I were interrogating. Furthermore, it was known to every British officer in and attached to the Allied Military Mission that GHQ in Cairo wished both ELAS and EDES to reserve their maximum efforts to coincide with Allied operations in support of the liberation of Greece. These were originally planned for April 1944 and were then postponed. Zervas therefore had good reason for not launching full-scale operations against the Germans – quite apart from his understandable preoccupation with ELAS.

Even so, the documentary evidence produced at the Nuremberg Military Tribunal[9] reveals that more was going on between Lanz and Zervas than met the eye – or at least my eye. It showed that on 18 December 1943 Lanz's headquarters received a message from the 104th Light Infantry Division in Agrinion stating that 'an officer authorized by Zervas personally has just offered serious cooperation and requests the German conditions by 19 December'. In addition, Zervas had two officers in Ioannina, Sarandis and Michalakis, in intermittent contact with Lanz's headquarters. On 4 January 1944 Lanz reported to the Chief of the General Staff Army Group E in Salonica that 'Zervas had requested for 18 January to have discussions concerning mutually fighting Communism. I intend to instruct Colonel Dietl to conduct negotiations without however concluding binding agreements.' A month later, on 3 February 1944, Lanz's staff were informed of Sarandis's offer from Zervas of 'efforts . . . for cooperation in the fight against Communist bands. Zervas will keep us constantly informed about his plans . . . he requires secrecy in this matter in order not to lose the supply deliveries from the Allies on which he depends. Zervas has refused all British attempts to make him cooperate with EAM.' On 9 February 1944 Gebhard von Lenthe, who was serving on the intelligence staff of XXII Mountain Corps, informed Army Group E in Salonica that Zervas's plenipotentiary had reported how EDES had profited from what amounted to if not a joint, a synchronized operation against ELAS on the eastern bank of the Arakhthos River: 'In the event of an allied landing, Zervas will take no action against the Germans, but will not resist the British

[9] F.O. 646, Box 345, Imperial War Museum.

either.' On 4 April von Lenthe received from Zervas's emissary a copy of the Plaka agreement, dated 29 February, which he duly forwarded to Army Group E in Salonica, with the comment that Zervas had acted in this way 'because of his loyal attitude to us and in order to deceive the British so as to comply with their demands and receive further supplies'. While there can be no particle of doubt that Zervas was wholly committed from first to last to an Allied victory, his naturally secretive and often devious methods of attaining his ends made it easy for his enemies and even some of his friends to describe him as duplicitous. The heart of the matter lay in the question of priorities. For Zervas, the first priority was EAM/ELAS. This conditioned his contacts with the Germans. EAM/ELAS returned the compliment by treating EDES as its principal opponent. Indeed, when during the 'First Round' of the Civil War, in October 1943, Pyromaglou had telephoned to ELAS to negotiate an armistice, the reply had come back – on Aris Velouchiotis's instructions – that 'Zervas was a greater enemy than the Germans'.

Another source of information of easy access were the 5,000 abandoned Italians in Epirus. Many of them were lorry drivers; others had been allotted more menial duties. In early March 1944 we were given a detailed account of the whole contingent being paraded in the main square of Ioannina and offered these two options: to continue to serve with the German forces but to be given non-combatant duties, or to surrender and be treated as prisoners of war. No more than a thousand chose the latter option, but the remainder continued to provide a pool of informers to our agents on military movements, ration scales (which were being severely reduced) and the location of store dumps. Their claims for services rendered rarely went beyond a packet of cigarettes.

By the end of March 1944 reports were reaching us from Ioannina, Arta, Agrinion, Preveza and Corfu with such regularity that my bank of sovereigns – which were the only recognized form of payment – was exhausted and I had to borrow eighty sovereigns from Tom Barnes, who on this and subsequent occasions regularly advanced me loans without comment, as he was on the receiving end of regular supplies on a scale far exceeding my own. The total cost of my mission, including our upkeep and food (mainly bought on the black market in Ioannina) and payments to our extended network of agents, now amounted to over a hundred sovereigns a month. The purchasing power of the sovereign fluctuated from week to week. In early April it was worth 35 million drachmae at a time when bread was costing 600,000 drachmae per *oka* (the equivalent of 2.8 lbs), beans 1.5 million, oil and rice 4 million and cheese 5 million. Payments to agents naturally varied, but on average they were receiving between four and five sovereigns a month, which by no standards could have been described as extravagant. What we were missing is apparent from a signal I sent in late March pleading that my next drop should include, flour, egg powder, jam, sugar, chocolate, macaroni, tinned sausages, tinned fish, dehydrated potatoes, yeast-vite tablets – and a special request for no more bully beef! But this in itself shows that we were far from starving.

After more than two months in Tseritsana it had become widely known throughout the area, largely due to tales spread by Costakis, in whose house I was staying, that the purpose of my mission was somewhat different from the other British officers attached to EDES under Tom Barnes's command. Consequently, Maniakis and I spent much of our time not only processing the information from our regular sources, but also in discussion with stray visitors who had heard of us after they had been to Zervas's headquarters in Derviziana. Thus an instructive day was spent by Maniakis in early March with a regular officer named Captain Ligerakis, the former EDES commander in the Zagoria area, who had been captured by ELAS at the start of the First Round in October 1943, and was released after the Plaka Bridge armistice in February 1944. During his captivity he had made friends with Captain Troianos, the ELAS commander in the Grevena area, and had learned from him how easily he had deceived British officers attached to ELAS about the number of men under his command and the area he controlled. The true figure of 4,000 men under Troianos's effective control was inflated to 6,000 when demonstrating his order of battle to SOE (and consequent need of appropriate supplies of arms and sovereigns). Troianos also took particular care to play down the role of the small, independent anti-Communist organizations like the PAO (Panhellenic Liberation Organization) in Macedonia, which he admitted were gaining popular support as a result of the most counter-productive and mistaken ELAS propaganda, which claimed that 'the Bulgarian people', who were universally detested, were opposed to their fascist rulers and therefore friends of Greece.

Another visitor handed on to me by Tom Barnes was Giorgos Baos, who had recently arrived from Athens with impressive letters of introduction from two pre-Metaxas Members of Parliament, one Liberal, one Populist. Baos, who had been educated in France and America, gave a damaging description of the EDES organization in Athens, which was not only partly German penetrated but was also flagrantly misusing its funds for the private benefit of its leading organizers. This news clearly embarrassed the Greek office, who advised me to have nothing to do with him in the future.

In mid April, when it was known that the Allied invasion had been postponed, reports reached us from Ioannina, Agrinion, Levkas and Corfu, all of which showed the sensible propaganda line being spread by the Germans through Epirus. Four main points were implied: that Stalin had persuaded Churchill and Roosevelt he should have the controlling hand in the Balkans; that, contrary to Allied expectations at the Teheran Conference in 1943, the Wehrmacht had not used up its reserve divisions in the Balkans; that Churchill and Roosevelt feared an Allied invasion of Greece would be the signal for the restart of civil war; and that HMG had fallen out with Tito and had been forced to renew relations with Mihailovic. But if this was the propaganda put out by Lanz, we also knew from a situation report prepared for him by his Chief of Staff, a copy of which was passed to us, that he was preparing for the eventuality of combined EDES/ELAS operations against his forces when the Allies landed in western Greece.

After four months' experience of mountain life in Epirus, the nature of my mission had begun to change in two ways. By living week after week in the exclusive company of Greeks and speaking my own language only when I was visiting Derviziana to exchange news with Barnes, Hamish Torrance, his deputy, and other members of the Allied Mission, I had begun to absorb the atmosphere and gain the confidence of those around me. Maniakis's help to me in this respect was invaluable. His open, cheerful character made him popular with every kind of person, no matter whether he was a senior EDES commander or a simple *andarte*. I saw that he had a natural gift for starting, continuing and expanding a conversation on virtually any subject under the sun. In this way I found myself participating more closely than most of my other compatriots in the arguments, jokes and gossip, which each day extended my understanding of what mattered most in their lives. In conversation with a prominent and popular EDES commander like Captain Zotos or with one of his men, the first things that struck me were their passionate interest in people and the overriding importance of their families. Personal friends and enemies were one thing, but their families were something sacred, the magnet that attracted the best of their energies and the last drop of their loyalty. Another striking characteristic was their unconditional commitment to the main causes for which we were all fighting, and an unshakable belief that both victory and better times were round the corner. At the same time I frequently heard expressions of both shame and bewilderment at the plight of their country, which was so profoundly divided. 'How is it possible', a senior EDES commander said one day, 'that we Greeks who were the envy of free Europe when we were fighting and beating the Italians in Albania, should so suddenly have transformed ourselves into wild animals at war with one another? What has happened to us? What caused this fundamental change. Perhaps we combine the best and the worst in human nature. If our eyes look up to the sun and the stars, our feet are in the mud.'

There was also a certain cynicism about at least some of their leaders in the eyes of many *andartes*, which was nourished by the ample evidence that the first prize for acquisition of rank and local power was the ability to distribute favours. I had learned very early on the significance of this important action – covered by the word *'rousfeti'* – which affected all forms of organization from the management of EDES at every level to the administration of the smallest village. Nothing could be achieved if you did not have 'the means'; with such means, there was little that was unattainable. Anywhere and at any time it was vitally important to know how to approach the person above you. This was indeed no special characteristic of Epirus or EDES, as I was quickly to learn when I was able to make contact with those who had been living in ELAS territory on the other side of the Pindus. It showed the intelligent reservations of the ruled about their rulers – regardless of the ideological split between EAM/ELAS and EDES. Indeed, the absence of any counter-ideology in EDES-controlled Epirus was strikingly evident.

The second way in which my mission changed was that, just when I was gaining confidence that I had absorbed enough to have something to report other than military intelligence, I was pleasantly surprised by the Greek office's request for an assessment of the political scene. This came without warning or any indication of why there had been this abrupt switch from my original instructions in Cairo to concentrate exclusively on German military information and leave the politics of the resistance severely alone.

In April 1944 I sent my first assessment to Cairo, which was based on my contacts with EDES officers and among the constant stream of arrivals in Tseritsana both from Epirus and the territory held by ELAS on the other side of the Pindus Mountains, which separate Epirus from Thessaly. I had also maintained contact with Pyromaglou on my regular visits to Zervas's headquarters in Derviziana. Our conversations showed his growing concern with HMG's support of the King and I sensed his nervousness at Zervas's ready acquiescence in British instructions, which were regularly relayed to him from Cairo by Barnes. If it was suspected at the time, it was not known (at least I did not know) that Zervas had agreed a year earlier, in March 1943, to change sides on the constitutional question. Pyromaglou's own republican beliefs, however, showed no sign of wilting. He estimated the ratio of royalists to republicans among the regular officers in EDES to be no more than 6:4. It was not surprising that he never mentioned to me any criticism of Zervas, but I was conscious of his dilemma. I also knew from Maniakis and other royalist officers that Pyromaglou's republican fervour had made him adversaries as well as allies.

This division of opinion on the constitutional issue seemed the plainest illustration of the fact that EDES could not be a positive political force after the Germans withdrew. Its cohesion stemmed from what it stood against. But even here there were complications, since the EDES organization in Athens, as Pyromaglou and others had admitted to me, was badly compromised by its collaboration with the 'Security Battalions', an armed anti-Communist police force operating under the joint orders of the Germans and the Quisling Greek government in Athens. A large bracket of negatives made EDES the only serious opposition to EAM/ELAS. But it was harder to define how the amalgam of political views within EDES could make it cohere as a political party in the aftermath of liberation. In particular, loyalty to Zervas was hedged with conditions. No one in my experience questioned the validity of his patriotic initiative when he took to the mountains in the summer of 1942. At the same time, all of his compatriots knew of his adventurous political past, which provoked such different reactions as approval, disapproval, forgiveness and indifference. Only Barnes seemed to take an honest soldier's view that it was irrelevant what Zervas had been in the past and pointless to speculate on what he might do in the future. For the present he was following Cairo's orders: which should absolve him from any form of criticism. No one else believed that if Zervas survived the occupation, he would demobilize either himself or his movement. But no one, so far as I could discern, was entirely sure in which direction he would turn. Their doubts were fortified by the uncertainty of HMG's intentions. This, above all, would be the decisive factor.

The hardest thing to assess was what was happening in ELAS territory on the other side of the Pindus Mountains. EDES propaganda about a reign of terror was unconvincing, and was not taken seriously outside the small coterie of those who believed blindly in Zervas. More persuasive to me was the information, however fragmentary it may have been, that I was able to glean from talking to recent arrivals in Epirus from Thessaly. My conversations with the newcomers to our territory taught me to understand what EAM had meant to them in the early days of its existence and why they had joined ELAS. When I had talked to a schoolmaster from Larisa, a shopkeeper from Lamia, a garage mechanic and a factory worker from Volos – among many others – I was struck by the near identity of their separate experiences and reactions at the start of the German occupation in 1941. They had all expected a lead to come from somewhere or that some signal would be given to which they could respond. In particular, they had anticipated that the Greek Army, which had been the pride of the nation in its victories over the Italians in Albania, would have begun without delay to organize some form of national resistance.

But nothing happened. No senior officer in any of the armed forces gave a lead and no one from the prewar political world emerged as a national name around which resistance could crystallize. This caused first surprise and later disgust. Then they heard of the National Liberation Front (EAM) – a splendid name – and rushed to join without a thought of who was behind it. 'Even if I had known at the time', said the schoolmaster, 'that the Communist Party had masterminded EAM, I would not have cared in the least. Someone had to take the first step and if it was the Communists, I would have said: Good luck to them, it shows they have the guts which all the others lack. In fact, I did not know who was behind EAM. I just knew there were some patriots who were at last providing some focus for our energies and some means of proving to ourselves and others that Greeks were no longer going to accept the presence of the Germans with folded arms. When I was told to leave Larisa and go to the mountains, I left my home and my family with the compensation that at last I was able to do my duty. In fact I was proud to have fought for ELAS and killed Germans. Although I have broken with them now, I must remember that it was EAM which first allowed me to live with a clear conscience.'

'I felt ashamed of myself doing nothing', said the garage mechanic from Volos, 'and watching the Germans boss my country. This would never have happened if we had had proper leaders in Athens. But we had no one. The first time I felt like a man was when my brother and I joined EAM and went to the mountains. Nor do I have the slightest regret now at what I did then. I fought the enemies of my country.' 'I was struck', said the shopkeeper 'by the fact that as soon as I joined EAM, I found myself part of a well-oiled machine. There was a miraculous communications system which whisked me off to the mountains as soon as I had proved my determination to take an active part and fight.'

83

In the beginning, no other resistance organization was in competition with EAM – as the stories of these admirable, unsophisticated people proved. At that stage of the occupation, it was clearly meaningless to level the charge against EAM that it was inflexibly determined to monopolize the business of resistance. That it greatly benefited from the efficient operation of the clandestine communications system of the Communist Party, which had been driven underground by Metaxas in 1936, was a fact that should only have been unwelcome to the Germans and their collaborators. By everyone else it should have been treated as a blessing. Later, of course, and notably after October 1943, it was quite plain that EAM/ELAS, under Communist direction, was carrying out its plans to eliminate all its rivals; from that time, at the latest, the charge of 'intent to monopolize at all costs' was justified. By then its grip on Free Greece outside Epirus was a fact; but it was no less a fact that a great many of those who were fighting with ELAS had originally enrolled for the best of reasons and the purest of motives. Only a few, such as those to whom I had had the opportunity of speaking, had either the skill or the luck to change sides. The schoolmaster had been forced into spreading primitive Communist propaganda about the new and so-called democratic Greece under the people's rule that would emerge when the Germans had been defeated. But he saw that if the people's rule, such as he witnessed in the mountains, was transferred to the towns, it would involve the brutal elimination of many of his innocent compatriots. This was not his understanding of the democratic process. The shopkeeper had fallen foul of the authorities because he had flinched and ultimately refused to kill a German prisoner in cold blood. The garage mechanic had baulked at giving evidence against a member of his family, who had been wrongly accused of collaboration with the Germans. But although their reasons for changing their minds about EAM/ELAS were different, none of them confirmed the wilder stories that were circulating at this time in Epirus of what it was like to live on the other side of the Pindus. I found it specially significant that they all still spoke with pride of the reasons why they had joined EAM in the first place. This made me reflect that if I had been in their shoes, I would have taken the same path.

'Morale is still high,' I signalled in my first political report on 27 April 1944

because everyone expects liberation in mid-summer. There has been natural disappointment, yet no despair after the recent postponement of the Allied invasion. What matters most is what will happen thereafter. There is universal apprehension of the immediate aftermath of liberation when it looks as if the towns will become the battlefields of what is now a mountain civil war. Public clamour is for the following things in this order: food, freedom from the German occupation and the minimum of security so that a semblance of democratic life may begin again. No political movement in free Greece is capable of meeting the last requirement. All armed political mountain parties engender differing degrees of mistrust. The King and the Greek Government in Cairo conjointly profit from being a theoretical alternative to the nightmare of future dominance by EAM/ELAS or the stark unreality of EDES as a national political organization. But support for the King and his Government in exile is highly equivocal since they have virtually no links with the resistance and seem out of touch with most of the realities of occupied Greece. The King, in particular, is a controversial figure whose past can be neither forgiven nor forgotten by traditional republican sympathizers in EDES, and is at least one of the root causes of support for EAM/ELAS. In any event HMG is held responsible for whatever the King or the Greek Government may do or say, since literally no one believes that any Greek administration – unless of course it is dominated by EAM – can or will act independently either now or immediately after liberation.

The transformation of EDES into a political party following the German withdrawal, can only be a fraud. Its record of collaboration with the Germans in Athens is only one of many severe complications. Barnes may try to create a Zervas legend, but it is not treated seriously by some of the best EDES commanders I have met like Papadatos, and Constantinidis. These are not the only ones who have informed Zervas that they will not support any of his political adventures after Allied liberation. Even some simple andartes are cynical about Zervas's political aspirations, but this is as nothing compared to their bewilderment at the state of our relations with ELAS.

It is widely acknowledged that Tito is pinning down more and better divisions than those which are now occupying Greece. Indeed there are a number of intelligent members of EDES who respect and even envy what Tito has achieved in organizing a genuinely national resistance in Yugoslavia. Although it is not understood why we are backing Tseta (the equivalent of ELAS) in Albania, our policy of support for Tito is approved, because it is realized that his is a nationalist movement which is at war with the Germans as the first enemy. It is not only in Epirus that the Germans profit by being the second enemy.

This is unfair because it is obvious that ELAS must have caused much more damage to the Germans than EDES, if only because it controls far more territory than Zervas will ever win to his side. The truth is that neither of the two opposed resistance movements, for which each is the first enemy of the other, has really got to grips with fighting the Germans. The tragedy of it all is that both ELAS and EDES have the same sort of Greeks in their ranks. It is lunatic to suggest that the only patriots are with Zervas in Epirus. But it is not lunatic to have the strongest suspicion that those who are resisting with EAM/ELAS in Thessaly, Macedonia and the Peloponnese are part of a political movement that makes EDES look innocent.

Three

By early May 1944, I and all those around me had begun to feel more relaxed as we approached the climax of the war and knew that we were on the winning side. The BBC broadcasts, which I followed on my small portable wireless set, kept us abreast of the news that I relayed each day to Costakis, who expanded his own and his neighbours' knowledge of geography. In this way the rest of the village learned how the Axis powers had been ejected from Africa and how India had been defended from invasion. There was now no danger to Australia and New Zealand since Japan was on the defensive. The Russian armies had expelled the German invaders and, as they well knew in Epirus, Italy was fighting on our side. The question was not if, but when the Allied armies would land in France, and when the Russian advance in Eastern Europe would force the Germans to retreat from Greece. In the first week of June the fall of Rome and the successful start of the Anglo-American landings in Normandy made us all speculate on the timing of Lanz's departure.

After living for months in the village, Tseritsana had become my home. We had begun to feel less isolated when it became possible for submarines to land stores and personnel on the coast near Parga and return to Bari with SOE couriers carrying, among other things, captured German documents and our private letters. At the first such opportunity I had written to my mother to explain how safe and happy I was in a mountain village 'where there is apple and cherry blossom and a breeze across the sun's rays pushing the clouds down the valley'. By hearing Greek spoken all day and sung for much of the night, I had acquired sufficient knowledge of the language to make myself understood, which allowed me to participate in more than the courtesies of life in the village. I was, of course, a stranger in their midst, but I had quickly noticed that Katsikakis, who came from Samos, and

Maniakis, from Levkas, were also described as *xenoi* ('foreigners'). The word covered not only those of non-Greek parentage but Greeks from any other part of Greece. Epirus, and especially the long beautiful valley of Lakka Souli, was a nationality to which no one had claim who had been born and brought up elsewhere.

About their own compatriots in the villages along the valley, they not only knew all that was to be known but were glad of any opportunity to parade their knowledge. In this way I was warned from the start to distinguish between the good and the bad in EDES and not to be fooled by appearances. A local commander on the other side of the valley two hours from Tseritsana began the practice of regularly coming to see me soon after I had arrived in the village. He asked no favours of me and I found him an agreeable companion. But after his third or fourth visit I was offered the news that he was misappropriating some of the sovereigns given to him to pay his men. I was even told the modest sum that was at first involved. Some three months later, Zervas sacked him. I was also told of a British officer and his wireless operator in EDES territory, who played the same tricks. Both survived, and it was not until the Germans had left and we were all in Ioannina that I saw with what good reason these allegations had been laid. Happily, Maniakis had a spotless reputation and my close association with him greatly helped to establish my own position in the village.

I was also learning to follow and adapt myself to the traditional customs, superstitions and habits that regulated the lives of all those around me. In these village communities, the power and influence of the Greek Orthodox faith was instantly apparent. Soon after my arrival in Plaisia, I had witnessed the annual celebration of the Epiphany on 6 January, when the priest made his rounds blessing each house by sprinkling the main room with a sprig of basil dipped in holy water, while the members of the household, men, women and children, stood in silence with bowed heads. In mid April 1944 I had joined in the Easter celebrations in Tseritsana – the first feast of the year in the Orthodox Church, thereby outranking Christmas – and had cracked red eggs, symbolizing the blood of Christ, with my neighbours saying in reply to 'Christ is Risen', '*Alithòs Anèsti*'.

On their name days, which were more important than birthdays, I followed the habit of calling on Costakis's friends to offer congratulations and wish them 'many years and may you live to a hundred'. I had learned to say no by raising my chin and eyebrows and clicking my tongue, and to spit when something lucky happened in order to steer clear of the Evil Eye. Reading fortunes in the dried grounds left in a coffee cup was an art that I was taught to respect, as well as the polite practice of clicking worry beads during conversation. But above all, I was made to feel the grip of their religion by watching everyone of all ages bow and cross themselves every time they entered the village church, kiss the holy icon and stand reverently in the presence of God. The sanctuary with the altar, where the priest presided, symbolized the world of the Holy Ghost. It was divided from the nave, which held the congregation, by the iconostasis, with its banks of icons, over which rose the dome with the image of the Almighty surveying the scene and representing the union of heaven and earth.

I used to make it a regular practice most mornings to walk down with Costakis's wife and daughter to the fountain under the trees by the church where the women – dressed in long black smocks to their ankles, their heads hooded in scarves, twisting on spindles sheep's wool and goats' hair into thread – would gather to draw water for the day under the watchful eye of the village priest. Here the daily gossip of the village was exchanged, and I could see what the war meant to these people whose metropolis was Ioannina. Most of them had not even seen the town, and the privileged few who had travelled that far were justifiably proud of their consequent knowledge of worldly matters: what the women looked like and how they dressed, the names of the shops and which taverna served the best food, what films had been shown at the cinema, the size of the houses and the money spent on their upkeep. When, as so often, the talk turned on these subjects, it would end with a sigh from those who had never seen Ioannina and the firm resolve to enjoy the fruits of victory there as soon as the occupation was over. Athens was a city so distant, so unknown and so foreign that it was virtually equated in their eyes with a capital like London. No one in the village had been there, not even the much-travelled Costakis. They had only heard tell of

how Athenians behaved and what they looked like; they concluded that they must be greatly different from themselves,
because so many of them 'had been to Europe'. This meant
London and Paris and nowhere else.

At the same time, there was the assumption, which was shared
no less in Athens than in mountain villages in Epirus, that Greek
affairs were at the centre of world events and the prime
preoccupation of our leaders. What does Churchill say about us
and how does he see things? These were questions that men,
women and even children would put to me with a regularity that
severely tested my powers of invention and contrivance. Occas-
ionally the very erudite would ask: What does Roosevelt think?
What sort of people are the Americans? Are they really your
brothers? How is it that they speak English, and do you
understand them when they do so? How do you tell an
Englishman from an American? 'What kind of a person is Stalin?'
the village priest once asked me, as if I was expected to reply from
personal knowledge, and, 'Why does the British Government
support atheists?' – which was, of course, more of a reference to
EAM/ELAS, however ill-founded, than to Soviet Russia. I was
looked upon as some kind of link with the outer foreign world
and was expected to be as knowledgeable about it as they were
about their own immediate surroundings.

It was also a question of power and influence. Everyone
believed – and rightly – that the future of Greece was an
exclusively British concern. No other nation could challenge our
monopoly of political responsibility, which was so glaringly
evident from the presence of British liaison missions to both
EDES and ELAS. The King was in London and the Greek
government was in British Egypt. In fact, when the *andarte*
delegation returned from Cairo in August 1943, they were joined
by the first American officer to serve in occupied Greece, but
thereafter and until December 1944 Washington gave no overt
sign that it wished to take over or even share the British role.
Although German intelligence, in moments of fantasy during
1943 and the first half of 1944, gave Stalin the credit for having
infiltrated some hundreds of Russian liaison officers into territory
held by ELAS, the truth was known on both sides of the Pindus
that there had been no Russian presence whatever until the end of

July 1944, when a military mission under Colonel Popov landed at Neraidha near ELAS headquarters in a Soviet aircraft based at Bari, which was normally used to communicate with Tito.

In such circumstances, it was understandable that in western Greece, at any rate, a British officer was reckoned to have the power and means of changing events by exercising his own authority or by appealing to his superiors to exercise theirs. Petitions to intervene in this or that dispute or requests for pressure to be brought to bear on Zervas were therefore normal occurrences in the daily life of the village. As, however, the purpose of my mission meant that I had to establish contacts as far from Tseritsana as the Ionian islands, I had in consequence to handle inquiries that stemmed from people I had not seen, in places I had not visited asking for my help in many different kinds of ways. One of our agents in Corfu, for instance, appealed to me to get his brother promoted in the bank where he was working, and he would certainly not have believed me if I had replied that it was beyond my power to influence appointments of this nature. On another occasion, I was asked to send word to the best surgeon in Corfu to operate for a reduced fee on the ailing mother of one of our best informers. From Preveza I once received a request for the next supply drop to my mission to include six woollen cardigans from London and six pairs of 'London leather shoes, size 42'. But if these were the normal favours to be prized out of a person like myself, who, it was assumed, had the means of meeting their requests, which were usually to promote the interests of their families, there were other occasions when I received appeals that showed up the fiction that the British were in command of the situation.

One such instance was the following letter, written in attractive English, which was brought to me by hand from the island of Levkas at the end of April:

Gentlemen English Officers,

I beg your pardon for the trouble I give you. But I hope you will be so kind as to excuse me. I don't have the honour of knowing you, you don't know me too. But however we are friends.

I am a small boy, fourteen years old and lame. We are two brothers. I have a mother and . . . who knows, perhaps I have too a father. Mister Maniakis will have spoken to you about the question of doctor Mellas, who has been captured by the men of EAM. This is my father. I am sure you just know all the details of our great misfortune. If I would speak perfectly well the English language, I could write to you much more. But I know only a few words. So I cannot express myself. I cannot tell you how much I suffer when I am thinking that my poor father is far away of us, two whole months, up at the mountains between a people who doesn't love him. They can beat and torture him every day, and not give him anything to eat and to dress himself. Though my poor father was always very kind to all the people here.

If I were older and able-bodied I could run up to the mountains and save my father. But now, as I cannot do anything else, than to weep every day and night, I thought to write this letter and pray you with all my heart to take care of my father. You yourself, that you are master of these both organizations, do try, please, to save my father, to get him with you at your shelter. He is a doctor and even an officer, and he loves you very much. Look after my poor father please.

This is really a great favour I beg of you. But what can I do. I am in despair and I am very poor and without parents. Dont you believe that is a great pity to become an orphan. Think of your fathers in England who are waiting with agony for your happy return and take pity on me, that I am waiting with the same agony for the return of my father.

I am sorry to trouble you so much.

I will be eternally your friend.

I thank you with all my heart and I hope you will answer me one day that my father is safe near you.

Your small devoted friend
SPIROS MELLAS

Levkas, 28.4.44

Maniakis explained to me that this small boy's father was the chairman of the EDES Committee in Levkas. While he was on a trip to report to Zervas's headquarters, Dr Mellas had been arrested by ELAS and later executed because of the position he held in EDES.

The key phrase, 'you yourself that you are master of these both organizations', was not the naive observation of a boy aged fourteen. It was the interpretation, shared by the vast majority of men and women of all ages in western Greece, of what had happened in their country since the resistance movement began in earnest with the destruction of the Gorgopotamos viaduct in November 1942. To witness the trust that was still placed in the word of the British authorities was both a moving and a disquieting experience. My disquiet grew from their faith in our stores of political skill and wisdom. To those around me, it was inconceivable that the British government would let them down by allowing the whole of Greece to slide into subjection to the Communist rule of EAM/ELAS. Churchill, it was confidently asserted, must have some solution up his sleeve. Such confidence embarrassed me, because I had to pretend they were right, when I knew very well the uncertainties that clouded the political outlook, and in consequence the reasons why such unqualified confidence in us was misplaced. However, it was on the immediate future that most conversations turned, rather than on recriminations over the past, since everyone knew that we were witnessing the tail end of the occupation.

One of the main signs that liberation was approaching was the increased frequency of supply drops to my mission. After the first mistake when my stores were sent to Zervas's dropping ground at Derviziana, the operational efficiency of the Greek office improved in this respect, and two drops were successfully carried out in April and early May. In the village these were treated as major events that put those around me in direct touch with the great world outside in which they had such a passionate interest. 'Churchill is sending us stores tomorrow night,' Costakis would announce, as if the operation had been personally planned from Number Ten Downing Street. There would then be a rush of applicants to be included in the reception party, since it was known from previous occasions that participation brought rich rewards. Indeed there was a fight for places, which even included the women. Technical arguments were advanced: Stephanos claimed that Nikos's mules were lame and untrustworthy; Nikos argued that Stephanos had no experience of such matters and was only interested in the prize-giving at the end of the affair. Ioannis claimed that he should be chosen before Vassilis because he was stronger and could carry a heavier load. Andreas then advanced his qualifications over all comers. In the end, when Costakis had selected the team and inspected the mules, Maniakis and I would split them into groups: the first for preparing the fires, which indicated to the pilot the area at which he should aim, the second for unpacking the containers, the third for gathering them up together with their parachutes, the fourth for loading the supplies on the mules and the fifth for dealing with an emergency, such as a parachute that landed a long way from the fires.

After we had detailed each man and woman to his or her particular duties, I would announce the expected time of the plane's arrival on the following night, which was always subject to confirmation during the early evening of the operation. The signal usually came through about six o'clock for a drop timed to take place not long after midnight. As soon as it was received, the word was passed quickly round the village and the reception party would be ordered to assemble with their mules in front of our house a good two hours in advance of the plane's arrival. We always allowed plenty of time for mishaps and the invariable delays caused by disputes over the composition of the group. Who would finally be responsible for the unloading? Which one would lead the mule train back to the village? And so forth. With much excitement we would then march down to the dropping ground below the church, which was about half an hour from our house, prepare the fires and begin the long wait for the blurred hum of our plane. As the time grew closer, all talk was in whispers.

On both the April and May drops, the plane arrived no more than twenty minutes behind schedule. The first person to hear it shouted the news and rushed to light the fires. As the plane came over us, the pilot flashed a prearranged signal; when he acknowledged my reply, we knew that the stores would be dropped the next time round. A few minutes later, six long containers were floating down to us. Everyone suddenly burst out singing to welcome their arrival, as if they were human beings. The parachutes collapsed as the containers pitched into the hard ground and there was a scramble to wrench open the containers, each of which carried three cylinders. After a good deal of shouting, these were then loaded on to the mules and we made our way up the hill and back to the village, where virtually everyone had stayed awake to witness the scene.

Sovereigns, clothing, medicine, a new wireless set, a plentiful supply of tinned food and whisky were then carefully unpacked and checked off against the lists that had been signalled to me the previous evening of what was due to be despatched. For me the most precious item was the packet of letters from my family and friends in London and Cairo, which I carefully put aside to enjoy in a quieter moment. Once everything had been unpacked, there was the traditional ceremony of distributing the spoils to each of the groups in the reception party. We handed out tinned food, which was considered to be a luxury, and cut up the panels of the parachutes, which were greatly valued by the women, who sewed the material into clothing for themselves and their men. Even the silk of the parachute cord was a prized possession. When each group had taken its share and Costakis was satisfied that no one had been forgotten, a hot meal was prepared and a party began that lasted till dawn.

Parachute panels were indeed a commodity that could be easily bartered and were the near equivalent of sovereigns. I took special care to ensure that they fell into the most deserving hands and always consulted Costakis over the distribution of this special favour. Before the drop in May, he had drawn my attention to the plight of an educated old man named Lazaros Khronis with whom I had often sat for a chat whenever I found him squatting on a stool outside his two-roomed house, leaning on his stick and staring sadly into space. Unlike some others, he had never asked me for anything and had never complained. But I could see from the rags he wore and his emaciated face that daily sustenance posed a special problem for him. Like many others, he was living on a few beans and *bobota* which was bread made from maize flour. I therefore welcomed Costakis's suggestion that he should head the list of beneficiaries after our next drop. He was, of course, too old and ailing to join the teams that went down to the dropping ground, so I personally delivered him his present the following morning. A tiny tear slipped out of one eye as he stood up to press both my hands in his without uttering a word. There was an anxious pause and then he said that he would write me a letter. Later that evening, there was a knock at my door and he handed me a folded piece of paper. 'I have written what I feel,' he said, and turned away. It translated as follows:

Dear Mr Jim,
 I find no words to thank you for your donation of four panels to my house. From the depth of my heart, I pray that all your wishes will be met and that the valiant efforts which our great Allies are making for the liberation of our poor country will receive their due reward. Your

gesture is most deeply appreciated. We would have been deprived even of bread if our Allies had not quickly sprung to our aid. I especially am not ashamed to admit that I would be starving because I own no mules, no plot of land or anything else. I have to live on my pension which amounts to the ridiculous sum of four million drachmae a month. You did us a great service because we had no means of buying either clothing or shoes. May God guide you safely back to your own home and may you live a happy and cloudless life.

With deep respect and always grateful

LAZAROS DEMETRIOS KHRONIS

As the drops became more regular and our supplies of food and drink increased, Spike Moran, with whom I had continued to keep in close touch, encouraged me to organize a few parties where he took the responsibility of providing the girls. He not only succeeded in mobilizing local talent, but such was his reputation in Ioannina, that an open-ended invitation from him would quickly lead during the following weekend to the arrival of a platoon of young people anxious to join in the fun. In this way, my house in Tseritsana also became known as the place where Spike Moran and Zotos, who was one of the best EDES commanders, gave their liveliest parties, which were considered a failure unless they lasted all night. To these celebrations, the flower and beauty of Ioannina, led by Aliki Kalphakakou and her sister (but chaperoned by their brother Panagiotis) and followed by many of their friends, would bravely make the seven-hour walk from the town on a Friday night in order to be in fighting trim on Saturday evening. There was a quaint air of respectability about all such parties, which were the opposite of debauches, but they provided the opportunity for us to relax and laugh and forget about the Germans for an evening. It also brought us into contact with every kind of gossip from the big city of Ioannina, which made it pellucidly clear to me that everyone knew who was working for whom. This was a further indication to me that it was unrealistic to expect secrecy in such circumstances.

As the Kalphakakou girls were daughters of a retired colonel, it was only to be expected that their thank-you letters to me and Spike Moran were punctually despatched by the same couriers who were carrying more important findings from our agents, and regularly ended with the deep respects and greeting from their parents, who had of course authorized their outings in the mountains. These gatherings also happily gave birth to romances: it was in this way that Mario Maniakis met and became engaged to Georgia Vakalopoulou in mid summer and later married her after the war, and that Leon Tsombos later married Loukia Polimenou. Our work had indeed made us into a family.

In the meantime, the military information reaching us during May 1944 became more detailed and abundant. In particular, by tracking the practice manoeuvres of XXII Mountain Corps, which were personally supervised by Lanz and Colonel Bürker, his Chief of Staff, we got warning of the German plans to make a drive against Zervas. When they decided to call off the drive through Epirus, we not only got the news through three independent channels from Ioannina – all of which were separate from EDES – but we also had the whole story of nervousness and confusion retailed to us in detail by deserters. Our interrogations revealed the low calibre of Lanz's troops. Sometime soon they would all be gone for good. This made it all the more urgent to attempt to gauge the political future and analyse the intentions of the Greek Communist Party.

My next opportunity to do so came in mid May, when a young lawyer from Ioannina named Christos Ifandis appeared in Tseritsana with an introduction to Maniakis from mutual friends. He had a personal tale to tell of political importance, which I recorded in the following report:

Ifandis was an early member of EAM and had attended the first secret conference in Athens in September 1941 at which EAM policy had been exclusively geared to national liberation. Soon afterwards he was posted to Ioannina to spread EAM propaganda in Epirus. In February 1942 his suspicions were raised after being contacted by two Communists from Athens who ordered him to adapt his propaganda, hitherto aimed only at national liberation, to Communist principles. This was his first indication of a policy switch, which was confirmed by his visit to Athens in the summer of 1942 when he learned that EAM was in touch with the Communist parties in Albania and Yugoslavia. He also heard that power within the Communist Party (KKE) was being shared between Siantos, as KKE leader dealing with the mountain resistance and Ioannides, as Organizational Secretary controlling the Party apparatus and the political struggle in the towns. He returned to Ioannina and faithfully carried out his instructions to plead the Communist cause. In October 1942 he was arrested by the Italians, sent to Italy and only returned to Epirus after the Italian armistice in 1943.

Still loyal to EAM, he travelled to Thessaly and Macedonia to bring himself up to date on what had been happening while he had been imprisoned in Italy. In all the local committees, but most blatantly in Salonica, he found that the joint directives from KKE, EAM and ELAS were to continue the camouflage of fighting for national liberation. Thereafter the party line emphasized that 'the people' would be free to choose their own form of Government. In fact the real aim of military victory was to achieve political power for the Communist Party (KKE). If there had been a chance for the so-called 'moderate' Communist leaders to make their voices heard, this was lost in the summer of 1943 when Tzimas was posted to Tito and Petros Roussos was set aside. This allowed Siantos to gain overall control and push forward his principal aim of ensuring EAM/ELAS control of the resistance movement as the essential prerequisite for the seizure of power in the aftermath of liberation. To this end, the Greek people needed 'education'. In October 1943 at ELAS Headquarters in Zagoria, he was shown a copy of a directive from KKE in Athens which made the following points: Britain and American were jointly responsible for Greek misfortunes. The Allies would never invade Greece; liberation could only come from Russia. With members of the British Mission, it was specially important to play up the fact that ELAS represented the Greek people in arms and was therefore a democratic army. It was no less important to play down, and if need be to deny Russian sympathies or influence. Above all British Officers should be deprived of their own contacts with Greeks, as far as possible.

In November 1943 when visiting the EAM Committee in Larisa he was informed of the plan to buy German arms with British sovereigns dropped to ELAS, which were to be hidden for future use in Larisa and Volos. In Salonica, he was shown a copy of the agreement with the Bulgarian Communist Party in July 1943 which allowed for an 'independent' Macedonia to extend over Thessaly as far as Volos. Nepheloudis, a leading Communist Trades Unionist in Athens, later confirmed to him that this was irrevocable EAM policy.[10]

During the mountain civil war in January 1944, Ifandis was in Athens where he learned that a joint KKE/EAM appeal had been made to Moscow for arms to fight 'Greek Fascism'. This had been coupled with the request that Russian influence should be brought to bear on Britain and America to convince them that ELAS was a 'representative' army like Tito's. The Russian reply was interestingly cautious, and all the more credible for that reason. It stressed that their approaches to the

[10] This so-called Petrich agreement was almost certainly a forgery.

Allies would be made conditional upon EAM's success in gaining the support of the official representatives of established Greek parties, especially the pre-war Liberal leaders and notably Papandreou and Sophoulis. Alternatively, if this failed, EAM was to try and foment trouble between them. Both in fact refused to co-operate with EAM in any way, Sophoulis going so far as to say that EAM was a pseudo-Bulgarian Party, and as such a worse enemy of Greece than the Nazis. When EAM/ELAS set up a shadow government on 14th March 1944 under the title of PEEA (Political Committee of National Liberation) and persuaded Professor Svolos, a Socialist, to be its Chairman, the communists succeeded in broadening the appeal of their national liberation movement, without in any way relaxing their grip on EAM/ELAS. The PEEA was charged with administering all the areas of Greece controlled by EAM/ELAS according to the principles of 'popular self government and popular justice'. But the interpretation of these principles was left exclusively to the KKE. When Ifandis saw what was happening, he resigned his membership of EAM; but not before he and others had learned of the shocked reaction of Siantos and Ioannides when Stalin ignored the existence of the PEEA and sent a telegram of congratulations to the King on 25th March (Greek Independence Day).

It was the setting up of PEEA that quickly led to changes in the Greek government in Cairo. On 26 March PEEA launched an appeal for a government of national unity, and on 31 March a group of officers from the Navy sent a petition to Tsouderos demanding a broadening of his government and recognition of PEEA. Tsouderos interpreted this move, which he knew to have some support in the Army, as an attempt by republican supporters in the armed forces to compel the King to accept that he should not return to Greece without a plebiscite. In order to avoid being forced from office, Tsouderos offered on 3 April to resign in favour of Sophocles Venizelos, the Minister of the Navy, who was the son of the Prime Minister in the First World War and founder of the Liberal Party. While these negotiations were proceeding, there were mutinies in the Army and the Navy on 6 April, which led to the King's arrival in Cairo from London on 11 April. With Churchill's support, he announced that the constitutional issue would be shelved until Greece was liberated. Tsouderos resigned on 13 April and was immediately replaced by Venizelos, who remained in office for less than two weeks. On 17 April, however, he was able to announce that EAM/

ELAS and EDES had agreed to send their representatives to Cairo. But on the same day, ELAS attacked EKKA, murdered its leader, Colonel Psarros, and promptly thereafter PEEA, ELAS and KKE demanded separate representation. Meantime, the mutinies continued and were only suppressed after British intervention had forced through the appointment of Admiral Petros Voulgaris to deal with the Navy and British troops had disarmed the 1st Greek Brigade. EAM/ELAS was held responsible for the mutinies, which failed to achieve any of their political objectives. In the subsequent reorganization General Constantine Ventiris formed the Mountain Brigade, which later won military laurels in Italy by capturing the town of Rimini and returned to Athens in November 1944: which elicited a protest from EAM/ELAS shortly before the fighting began in December.

On 26 April Venizelos resigned and was replaced, to Ambassador Leeper's great satisfaction, by George Papandreou, the leader of the small Democratic Socialist Party, an offshoot of the main Liberal (Venizelist) Party, who had just emerged from Athens. It was he who convened the so-called Lebanon Conference which took place from 17 to 20 May. All the prewar political parties, which had been suppressed by Metaxas's dictatorship in 1936, as well as all the resistance movements, were represented.

This was an event of the first political importance. When I pressed the Greek office to be kept fully informed of the proceedings of the Lebanon Conference, I received a summary of the four-day debate in under ten lines. Fortunately, I had no need to press for something more informative, as a copy of the official record of the Conference was passed to me by Boulis Metaxas, who with his father, Colonel Stavros Metaxas, and Pyromaglou, had been the EDES representatives. I had a long and friendly discussion with them on their return from Beirut. Pyromaglou, running true to form, took this opportunity to give me a detailed description of the personalities and performances of the prewar parliamentary members of the Liberal, Populist, Progressive, Agrarian and Communist Parties (which advanced my political education) in addition, of course, to providing a vivid commentary on the speeches of Miltiades Porphyrogenis, the Secretary General of EAM, and Saraphis, who spoke for ELAS.

The official record showed that in his opening address on 17 May, Papandreou did not mince his words. 'It is the responsibility of EAM', he said,

that they looked beyond the struggle for liberation and were preparing in advance for their own domination after the war. Their first aim was to monopolize the national resistance. Indeed they had made themselves into a State within a State. The terrorist activity of EAM/ELAS had enabled the Germans to achieve in the third year of the occupation what they had failed to effect in the first two years: the creation of the Security Battalions whose aim was internal strife. In this way, a vicious circle has been created. Andarte bands, national organizations and the Security Battalions are neutralized by each other. The help which the Allies are giving is almost in vain. Only the Germans succeed in remaining aloof and mock ironically at the Greeks and their allies. The only way to escape from this vicious circle is to form a National Army. But this means that EAM must abandon its designs of domination by force.

This speech was followed by others from Liberals, Populists and Progressives, who reiterated the same theme and set the stage for the subsequent shouting match between EDES and EKKA on the one hand, and the Greek Communist Party (KKE), EAM/ELAS and the PEEA representatives, Professors Alexander Svolos and Angelos Angelopoulos, on the other. One of the most telling interventions came from Kartalis speaking for a disbanded EKKA, following the recent murder of Colonel Psarros by ELAS. He pinpointed the stages by which EAM had progressed toward its aim of general domination of the resistance movement and quoted a remark made to him by George Siantos, the Secretary General of the Greek Communist Party that 'everyone who is not in EAM belongs to the Gestapo'. Unsurprisingly, the EAM/ELAS representatives replied with no less vigour and accused both EDES and EKKA of collaborating with the Germans. The Conference ended with the proclamation of the Lebanon Charter comprising the formal agreement that 'all guerrilla bands in free Greece must be unified and disciplined under the order of a single government', and that a 'national' government was to be formed with five vacancies left for EAM. But it was hard to believe that any such administration could work or would last, or that any solution had been found for any of the fundamental problems that gripped the two main resistance movements. Pyromaglou spoke admiringly of Papandreou's performance. He seemed pleased that the newly appointed Chief of the Greek General Staff, General Ventiris, was a staunch anti-Communist Venizelist like himself; but he also thought it both wise and fair that other key military appointments, such as that of Colonel Thrasyvoulos Tsakalotos, who took command of the Mountain Brigade, should have been awarded to royalists.

After analysing with Pyromaglou the results of the Lebanon Conference, I sent a further commentary to the Greek office on Ifandis's report saying that it provided some of the background and confirmation of the reasons for Papandreou's stand. I stressed again the German advantage of being classed as the second enemy, pointing out that, in Epirus at any rate, Lanz's propaganda problem had been considerably simplified. He should have derived much comfort from the comment that had been frequently reported to us from Ioannina: 'If the Germans win, we have lost Thrace [to Bulgaria]; but if EAM/ELAS wins, we have lost Greece.' I also gave a brief sketch of the difficulties I was encountering – it was becoming an almost daily experience in the village – in trying to explain and, indeed, to justify British policy toward ELAS. On my regular trips to Derviziana, which I visited about once a week to report my findings to Tom Barnes and Hamish Torrance and to exchange news and views with Zervas and Pyromaglou, I found my powers of advocacy under increasing strain.

No one questioned how or why we had become involved with both EDES and ELAS from the start of their joint venture in the Gorgopotamos operation in 1942. What seemed inexplicable, not only to those who gathered every day round the village fountain in Tseritsana but to as sophisticated an observer as Pyromaglou, was why Allied support for ELAS had not been progressively reduced throughout 1943, since we, the British, still controlled the powerful lever of supply. Although no one knew better than Pyromaglou that after the Italian collapse in September 1943 the arms and equipment of General Infante's Pinerolo Division had been exclusively acquired by ELAS, he and a number of other EDES commanders remained in no doubt that 'some magical means' could and should have been found to keep ELAS short of arms. This was a further sign of the conviction of virtually everyone in Epirus that the British government held all the cards but was curiously unskilled at times in playing a winning hand. What I found hardest of all to manage was the lack of understanding as to why we had not made a clean break with ELAS, seeing that it was a flourishing resistance movement that controlled most of free Greece outside Epirus. For this indeed was the reality of the extent of its power. But as EAM/ELAS was likely both to survive and thrive, even in the event of the British missions being withdrawn (which was under consideration in June), I had no snap answer to the charge that Myers and Woodhouse had failed at an early stage to assess correctly the political and military consequences of maintaining support for a Communist-dominated resistance movement.

In fact, this charge against either or both of them was completely unfounded. But at that time I had no knowledge of the problems Myers had encountered in Cairo and, especially, in London in his dealings with Churchill. I had only met Woodhouse once in the company of other members of the Allied Military Mission and had had no opportunity of a detailed discussion with him, although I had been instantly impressed by his grip of the political situation.

My report concluded with the observation that the problem of British support for Greek Communists was sharply distinguished from the policy we were pursuing with Tito and from the broader issues of the Anglo-American alliance with Russia. This latter was understood and accepted, even if it was widely believed that it was a grandiose military expedient that would not survive Hitler's defeat. The Greek office in Cairo, which continued to relay GHQ's appreciation of the military intelligence I was sending, made no comment on either this or my earlier political report.

During April and May I had noticed that our traffic reports covering the Ioannina-Arta road were showing a certain pattern of movement. I therefore suggested to Zervas, with whom my liaison was becoming closer, that we should put our intelligence to use by breaking up the columns which regularly passed the watcher's post just before sundown. He agreed and a well-armed group was sent to the road. This minor operation worked well. A German convoy was taken completely by surprise and offered virtually no resistance. In a few minutes of shooting we destroyed all their transport and came back with ten willing prisoners. Three, who spoke no German, were from Turkestan and wore armbands with the inscription *Biz Alla Bilen*. The others were Volksdeutsche, mostly Poles or Alsatians, who were interrogated separately by Maniakis and myself. All of them were volubly anti-Hitler. Indeed two of them claimed that they had shot their officers in the back at the moment the column had been stopped. A chance like that was something they had been waiting for, but they all emphasized that their own feelings, while widely shared among other ranks in their battalion, most certainly did not apply to the officers and NCO's. All of them said they had been told to expect Allied landings in western Greece in the very near future and that in that event they would be fiercely opposed. Not one of the seven had even an elementary knowledge or understanding of the Greek political situation in Epirus. Their officers had told them nothing, apart from occasional vague references to 'Communist guerrillas', who were armed by the British, and 'Greek nationalists', by which they meant the Security Battalions under German direction in Agrinion. None of them knew of Zervas or Saraphis or Aris Velouchiotis by name, or of EDES or EAM/ELAS, and they had heard nothing of the work of British liaison officers on either side of the Pindus. Two of them said they had been told to discount stories of British officers in the mountains as typical Communist trash. These interrogations indicated the quality of at least some of the troops under Lanz's command.

In late May and early June Zervas pressed a number of other minor attacks and came back on each occasion with prisoners who responded without pressure to interrogation. I was anxious to learn how Lanz was reacting to this short burst of activity, so I made an urgent inquiry from our link to Lanz's interpreter. He was able to pass us the latest intelligence assessment, which had been submitted to Lanz. This described the British objective to be the maintenance of an equilibrium between ELAS and EDES so that when the Allied forces reached Greece, we could impose any regime of our choosing. It concluded with the confident expectation of a second full-scale civil war between EDES and ELAS, and consequently the strong recommendation that this would be the moment to destroy both resistance movements. Zervas's renewed attacks were described as 'ill-advised' and explained away as being the result of British pressure on him at Derviziana. The whole tone of the report referred to Zervas more in sorrow than in anger, but it concluded with the assumption that he would find means of disregarding British pressure and advice and at least exploit the tactical advantages open to him, if the German offensive was initially launched against ELAS.

In fact, the German intelligence appreciation was rehearsing an academic argument because in the first week of June we had firm information that XXII Mountain Corps had been ordered to make a drive against Tseta, the Communist partisans in southern Albania. In particular, this meant the diversion of the 1st Mountain Division and in consequence Lanz's counter-attack against Zervas never materialized. Zervas took quick advantage of this situation to step up his harassing operations, which resulted in a further flow of prisoners and deserters who showed a steadily deteriorating level of morale. By the end of June, when the 1st Mountain Division came back from its successful anti-guerrilla operation in southern Albania, Lanz switched it almost immediately, on the orders of the Army Group in Salonica, into a large-scale attack against ELAS, centred on Pendalofos, in the northern Pindus. From the networks of informants organized by both Kalousis and the Cherub team, we received clear information that this operation, code named 'Steinadler', would involve all the best troops under Lanz's command. Profiting from its fresh experience in southern Albania, the 1st Mountain Division inflicted very heavy casualties on ELAS in the northern Pindus and the Grammos Mountains. Clear indicators of this German victory also reached us when the 1st Mountain Division returned to Ioannina in early July. The signs were that Operation Steinadler had been carried out on a scale far exceeding any previous attack on ELAS and had been much more carefully planned than any operation ever launched by Lanz against Zervas. When reviewing this operation in his 'Partisan Warfare in the Mountains', Lanz estimated that 'the bulk of three partisan brigades had been destroyed'. At the time we did not know these details, but it was safe to assess that after its exertions the 1st

Mountain Division was in no fit state to launch another major operation in the immediate future. The odds therefore against an attack on EDES had considerably lengthened, and could be discounted in the weeks ahead.

This seemed the moment for Zervas to strike even harder, and I welcomed the urgent call I received from him and Barnes to come to Derviziana and discuss the military options open to EDES. By the time I reached his headquarters, I found that the decision had been taken to plan a series of offensive operations. We could all see that this was the time for Zervas to assert himself militarily and exploit every chance of extending his hold on Epirus. It was also the time to begin to prepare the ground for the arrival of British troops. I therefore sent a long signal to the Greek office, which I cleared with Barnes, saying that we both considered I should begin to gather information of a different character, particularly on the economic situation. If, however, my brief was to be extended in this way I said that I would need another wireless operator to carry the additional traffic.

It was a happy surprise when I received a quick and positive response from the Greek office. In mid July a British wireless operator named Dennis Mulholland, who had been given proper technical training and brought with him the same type of set used by all the SOE missions (both these advantages had been denied to Katsikakis), was sent in by sea from Italy, where a regular boat service bringing stores, arms and ammunition had been in operation since June. The punctual arrival of these landing craft at fixed rendezvous and the efficiency of the EDES reception committees were indicators of increasing Allied superiority and, by the same token, of Lanz's weakening grip. Mulholland also brought with him a sensible economic questionnaire and, most important of all, a sufficient supply of sovereigns to keep my mission solvent for the next two months, which released me from the embarrassing obligation of asking for loans from Tom Barnes. My total expenditure over the last three months from April to June had averaged around 130 sovereigns a month, of which more than half was taken by the growing number of agents who were supplying our information. Indeed, the exchange value and purchasing power of the sovereign was one of the first points on which I was asked to report. In my reply, I felt I might have been recording what had happened in the Weimar Republic. When I arrived in December 1943 the sovereign had been worth 2 million drachmae. In early June 1944 it was 100 million and by the end of June 140 million. By mid July it was worth 260 million. In a later report I gave it as 340 million by the end of July. This bought about 5 lb of olive oil. In mid August the sovereign had risen to 780 million and by the end of August it was nearly 3 billion. We also had separate reports from Ioaninna and Preveza that Greek notes were being printed in Munich and issued to selected currency dealers to buy up sovereigns on the black market. In Preveza such trade was openly conducted by the Germans themselves without intermediaries. As the commonest denominations were ½ million, 1 million and 5 million drachmae, it was impossible for Greek banks to check or estimate the extent of this German infusion of Greek currency.

Without the extra wireless operator I could not have reported half the information at our disposal in July, especially when Zervas's operations in the Preveza area began to produce officers in his net of German prisoners. Their willingness to talk showed even more clearly that they belonged to a beaten force. On 17 July Zervas occupied Parga on the coast and on the same day we received independent reports from both Kalousis and the Cherub group that von Lenthe, on the intelligence staff of XXII Mountain Corps, had quoted Lanz as being mystified why Zervas was operating effectively against the Germans in the absence of an Allied invasion. On 25 July Kalousis reported that SS General Sedner had arrived from Athens and had made a joint approach with Lanz to Colonel Tarsakopoulos, the head of the Greek gendarmerie in Ioannina, to inquire how he would react if the Germans sought their cooperation in full-scale operations against Zervas. Tarsakopoulos gave the firm reply that if the Germans proposed to step up their operations against EAM/ELAS, the gendarmerie would continue the same degree of cooperation as hitherto, but in no circumstances would assistance be forthcoming for operations against any 'nationalist' organization, least of all EDES. These negotiations were monitored by Lanz's chief interpreter and a full account reached us two days later with the important postscript that, after the failure of these preliminary negotiations with Tarsakopoulos, Sedner had encouraged Lanz to send a deputation to Zervas demanding that he should break off relations with the Allied Military Mission. If, as was expected, Zervas refused point blank, it was proposed to offer him a truce, at least until the start of Allied operations in Epirus. I carried this information to Barnes myself, as I felt sure that Zervas would be receiving his own version of these negotiations from the EDES Committee in Ioannina. Barnes told me that he had heard nothing to this effect from Zervas and doubted the authenticity of our reports. Unless I could provide supporting evidence, Barnes said that he would not take this matter up with Zervas, and he specially asked me to make no independent approach to either Zervas or Pyromaglou. I agreed, on condition that we should review the situation again if I received corroborative evidence of German plans to negotiate with EDES.

In the last week of July I began to report the start of the German withdrawal, as the first contingent of Lanz's troops began to pull out of Metsovo and make their way up to Albania. So low was the state of morale, notably of the 104th Light Infantry Division, that Lanz made a special plea for reinforcement by the 4th SS Panzer Grenadier Division, which began to arrive in Ioannina from Volos on 28 July. It was this SS Division that slapped a curfew on the town from 8.30 p.m. until dawn. But our couriers had little difficulty in maintaining contact with us. With the continued advance of the Red Army in Eastern Europe and the progress of the Anglo-American invasion of Normandy since June, no one now doubted that we were witnessing the beginning of the end.

Four

It was at this juncture that the Greek office confirmed the radical change of its original position by asking for an extensive political assessment of EAM/ELAS to be sent out by safe hand. This was no problem, as the landing craft, which had been making the quick trip from Italy to the coast of Epirus and back since June, were functioning so regularly that we called them the Cook's Travel Service.

I welcomed the questionnaire that was signalled to me on 28 July 1944; but at the same time I was astonished by the evidence of the continued naiveté and ignorance in the Greek office of the conditions under which my mission had been operating for the past seven months. The signal read as follows:

Herewith directive on EAM. Objective information urgently required on aims and organisation of EAM/ELAS. All our Greek sources are prejudiced, but you are able to report faithfully views expressed to you by EAMites. Try to get members of all ranks and classes, especially but not only those in positions of trust and authority, to talk about their ideas of organization and their objectives. Subjects of particular importance are attitude to Greek Government in Cairo; possibility or otherwise of collaboration with them; intentions in case of Allied landings; attitude to British, Americans, Russians, Bulgars, Yugoslavs and Albanians, particularly in relation to possible collaboration with their left-wing organisations. Important to try and distinguish between expressions of genuine opinion and attempts to propagandise you.

My reply was sent on 10 August and reached the Greek office three days later, carried by an SOE officer in a sealed package with a stack of German documents and paybooks from prisoners who had been captured in the EDES operations during July.

The views I expressed were naturally my own. I had, however, learned a great deal, and in consequence been much influenced by many discussions during the summer, on my regular visits to

Zervas's headquarters, with two of the Greek interpreters attached to Tom Barnes's mission. The first was Alkaios Angelopoulos, who had been a foreign correspondent for the Beaverbrook press in Spain and Abyssinia before the war. He had an infinitely wider experience and deeper understanding of what was going on around him than any of the SOE officers. The other was Dimitrios Papaioannou, who joined the Diplomatic Service after the war and became Greek Ambassador in Madrid and Paris. He, too, was an acute observer who could take an equally detached view of the performance of both his own and my compatriots. Angelopoulos and Papaioannou were close friends and I made it a habit to talk things over with them whenever I had the opportunity to do so. It was their company above all others that I sought when I was in Derviziana. With them I felt more at home and more in focus than with any of the British officers. With Barnes, I never had a cross word and was always conscious of the multifarious forms of help he had given me to set up my mission and keep it going. But I had learned not to expect much from him, apart from a parade of Zervas's virtues, when evaluating the political outlook. In contrast, whenever I found myself with Angelopoulos and Papaioannou, we instantly got down to business, swapped news and views and talked and laughed through half the night, because happily there were often better things to do than discuss the politics of the Resistance. All three of us spoke freely and often disagreed: which showed we were friends. But basically, there was little difference between us when we tried to assess the way in which events were likely to develop in the immediate future. My regular contacts with Kominos Pyromaglou, whose republican fervour seemed to grow each time I talked to him, had also helped to shape my political views.

In my report to Cairo on 10 August 1944, I wrote:

I am glad to be able to answer your questionnaire by letter and thereby explain some of the political problems here in greater freedom than would be possible in encoded signals. First, I must clear up a curious misunderstanding. You asked about my personal contacts with members of EAM. How do you suppose that such contacts could exist in territory held by Zervas? Since the Plaka Bridge Agreement in February, which theoretically ended the civil war between ELAS and EDES, the only ELAS-ites crossing the frontier have been shot forthwith. Somewhat naturally, ELAS has reciprocated this form of hospitality. This may explain why I do not get leading members of EAM/ELAS knocking at my door for a drink and a confidential chat. Furthermore I would doubt if any British officer is in this privileged position. I trust that you were not fooled by what recently took place in Zagoria when we all knew that ELAS, on EAM's orders, mounted an operation to explain to a number of British officers how sweet, reasonable and innocent were the 'true aims' of their movement. It is common knowledge here that this carefully concerted Party line, which turned the truth upside down, was faithfully relayed – doubtless in good faith – by the British officers concerned. EAM was thus portrayed as being in favour of a 'truly democratic Greece' governed by nineteenth century liberal principles which would lead the country to have 'natural' links with the Anglo-Americans and with Russia. Passing references were, of course, made to the enemies of the people, who would be judged in the people's courts by the representatives of the people. When such questions were put as: What is the attitude of EAM/ELAS to the King and the Greek Government in Cairo?, the rehearsed reply was as follows: 'The King has stated on numerous occasions that he will not return unless or until his people want him back. The same obviously applies to his Government. We are an organisation designed solely to represent and carry out the people's interests. Indeed we are the only organisation so designed. You cannot call EDES, which holds an oppressive control over not even the whole of Epirus, an organisation which represents Greece. If the British Isles were occupied and a Fascist organisation was established in Wales, in opposition to a movement covering England, Scotland and Ireland, you surely would not call the Welsh organisation "British". The other organisations are either tiny independent growths, which are therefore irrelevant to the meaning of the word representation, or else they are offshoots of our own movement and hence already under the people's control. The people's representatives, voicing the people's interests, are decided on both issues of the King and the Papandreou Government. Neither are wanted back. As neither will return in opposition to the people who they fraudulently claim to represent, it is obvious that both had better remain where they are now.'

The crux of the whole matter is the simple distinction between the interests of the people and their so-called representatives. EAM never did want and never will want their bluff to be called. Although they can probably depend with some confidence on most officers in ELAS, the allegiance of the rank and file is another question. How otherwise can the desertions to Zervas be explained? Though never on a large scale, they come dribbling in, and it is also a fact that for several months now volunteers have joined EDES from all parts of Greece. Both sides pressgang for reinforcements from their own areas.

The so-called moderate elements in EAM/ELAS, which I gather have become a byword in Cairo, naturally exist though their importance should not be overrated. Among such moderates are at least four groups: those that having grasped the real objectives of EAM, disapprove of or are disgusted by the organisation, but for good reasons of fear for their own skins and those of their families, can and will do nothing about it. Then there are those who believe that EAM's objectives are largely figments of Zervas's imagination and that to gain sympathy and support for his own cause – particularly with the British – he has had to paint EAM/ELAS very much more red than it is in fact or aspiration. A third group consists of those who think that where there is smoke there is fire; that EAM's case against Zervas may be overpitched, but it is grounded in truth. The constant assertion that he is the Greek parallel of Mihailovic and has been 'collaborating' with the Germans, has made some of this mud stick. Finally, there are those who are in EAM/ELAS for what they can get out of it. I attempt no estimate of numbers in these groupings, except to guess that the last is probably the smallest.

EAM's aims are, I think, not difficult to understand if you live in mountain Greece. The secret is that their objectives are not secret. It is strikingly obvious that EAM is an organisation designed to obtain absolute political power in the aftermath of Allied liberation by any means deemed necessary in the circumstances. Any more polite and especially more 'liberal' way of putting the case castrates the truth. Anyone who knew anything about EAM before the Lebanon Conference has been consistently unsurprised by what has happened since May. If there had been any question of their cooperative participation in Papandreou's Government, it would only have been explained as a means whereby EAM saw a tactical advantage in being represented in the enemy camp. Genuine co-operation would have been inconceivable. EAM stands for everything or nothing. It will gain or lose all. This is why the issue whether a member of the Communist party, like Petros Roussos, will or will not join Papandreou's Government does not indicate whether EAM's policy is changing. Their tactics may change, but their strategy will not. Mercifully, Papandreou appears to be the last person to be deceived or to suppose that the problem of EAM is soluble by striking a bargain over a number of portfolios. If EAM does enter his Government, it could be because they wish to postpone the moment to strike. An alternative variant could be that EAM would then denounce their representatives as Trotskyists. We heard of preparations for this in June.

The answer, therefore, to your questions about the possibility or otherwise of EAM's collaboration with Papandreou's Government is almost disturbingly simple. Genuine collaboration never was and never can be within the furthest bounds of possibility. Participation for tactical reasons is a quite different matter. If EAM has succeeded in fooling the Foreign Office – after failing to fool Papandreou – into believing that it is an organisation which can dovetail into a national structure, then they have gained a victory of infinitely greater importance than their early successes with some members of the British Mission. In that event, an unparalleled disaster will descend on Greece for which HMG will carry the full responsibility. Those who live with ELAS are obviously best qualified to answer your question as to how their protectors will react to Allied landings. How could I add to their local knowledge? Living in Epirus, all I know is that British Missions to ELAS are prepared to beat it to Epirus if Allied landings result in ELAS's active hostility. This clearly cannot be dismissed out of hand.

I do not fancy that there is anything particularly abstruse about EAM's attitude to ourselves, the Americans and the Russians. In their eyes the Anglo-Americans – that is how they always refer to us, without imagining that there may be differences – represent plutocratic capitalism; we are therefore aligned with the enemies of the people and of the people's representatives. I have sent you printed propaganda showing clearly enough, I would have hoped, that EAM has drawn its sword and slashed us in the face. Byron's grave in Missolonghi, Navarino, Venizelos, Lloyd George and a hundred other things that make the huge majority of Greeks 'pro-British' almost beyond reason – to them all this is sentimental trash. On English soil, as Marx has shown, capitalism flourished to a degree not comparable with any other state in Europe. What possible alliance can exist, they say, between the declared enemies of communism and its disciples? The fact that EAM has never found its anti-British propaganda contagious is another issue altogether. When it comes to the crunch, the Anglo-Americans will be on the other side of the fence, they say, and classed – in every sense of the word class – with our enemies.

EAM looks to Russia as would any political movement that wants to relive the October, not the February, Revolution of 1917. The Bolsheviks and assuredly not the Mensheviks are their heroes. The reasons why EAM has so openly committed itself to take power by an imposed revolution are as mysterious to me as to many others. It is the worst and probably the most self-defeating policy to adopt in a situation where the country is aching for peace and security. I believe, furthermore, that if the Central Committee of EAM had been more astute, it could have deceived an even greater number of Greeks. As it is, EAM will be destroyed by its own propaganda. In general, however, you may be sure that EAM looks to Stalin with the same measure of admiration and trust as the rest of Greece looks to Churchill and Roosevelt. One side or the other will dominate in a clash that is believed to be inevitable.

To its geographical neighbours, EAM has formed the unsurprising policy of seeking support among friends. Now that it is BBC news that ELAS bands are with Tito, there is the answer in a line to the extent of their collaboration with fighting Yugoslavs. Even to EDES, this is the least dangerous aspect of EAM/ELAS's foreign relations. Tito, as I have already reported, is recognised as the leader of a Yugoslavia fighting with desperate success against the Germans. They may fear Tito, but at least they understand why we support him. With Tseta (their comrades in arms in Albania), ELAS has always been in the closest possible contact. I have sent several reports giving, I hope, the evidence of this. In sharp contradistinction to EDES, EAM completely opposes Greece's traditional claims on Northern Epirus (Southern Albania). But EAM's most serious and most puzzling foreign alliance is with the Bulgarians. You know what Greeks feel about Bulgarians – and indeed with what good reason. Yet EAM's line is still to stick to the old-fashioned dogma that 'only the Fascist Government in Sofia is to blame. The Bulgarian people are our comrades in arms.' On this point, they are inflexible. You must know that this would have been enough to ruin any cause in Greece. How could it have been believed before the war? How can it even be mentioned after the Bulgarian occupation of Thrace?

It would, of course, simplify matters and make the present situation clear-cut, if nationalist Greece was to a man united around EDES. This is unfortunately not so. Outside Epirus, where has Zervas found support? Even inside Epirus, it is not difficult to criticise him. But whatever charges may be levelled against EDES, the most unfounded is EAM's description of the movement as fascist and therefore the first enemy after the Germans have gone. EDES reverses the charge with the claim that a Communist-dominated EAM/ELAS, committed to a bid for power in the aftermath of the German retreat, constitutes the first enemy. The tragedy is the Communist dominated leadership of EAM/ELAS; by comparison, the leadership of EDES is merely a minor misfortune. Its best officers are its most exacting critics and would smile at Tom Barnes's attempts to canonise Zervas. It is all too true that if you took the gold out of EDES the body would have a damaged bone structure. But even so, it stands now and will always be remembered as the core of resistance against the first enemy in Greece. The heroes and the victims on both sides of the conflict between EAM/ELAS and EDES are the mass of the andartes, not their leaders.

We can hardly be expected to look at it this way now, and perhaps we never will. For anyone to find an enemy superior to Hitler is intolerable to our way of thinking and wholly unacceptable to our political purposes. But to the Greeks, the enemy within the country, who stays behind after the completely inevitable withdrawal of the Germans, must outrank all others. With our recent triumphs, the German forces are being regarded with more contempt than fear. They had the Italians in Epirus for two years. Then they collapsed and disappeared. In a matter of months, everyone believes that the Germans will be gone for good. EDES will then, I think, shrivel; but EAM/ELAS will remain intact.

Their immediate objectives reveal what they have in mind to do in the wake of the German retreat. There is much evidence to show that EAM's version of mountain justice will soon be brought to the towns. The recent incident at Amphilokia when they murdered a selection from their list of the 'people's enemies' gave a preview of what lies ahead. In Ioannina, I am informed that there are just short of a thousand on their black list. I have no figure for Preveza yet, but I know they are gathering data. In Agrinion, not only because of the Security Battalions, who are of course collaborating with the Germans and deserve no mercy, EAM is also preparing a blood bath.

At this time a number of political reputations are being revised. The first of course, is Metaxas. It is rare to hear praise of the 4th August, 1936, but many of those who opposed Metaxas for the best reasons now grudgingly grant him credit for his anti-communist fervour. Quisling Prime Minister John Rallis too may profit from 'the first enemy'. When his name comes up, a typical conversation in Epirus often turns this way: 'What are his crimes as a Greek? To have been head of a collaborationist Government which stained the name of Greece abroad – this no one can deny. But what are his crimes in Greece to Greeks? If the answer is the Security Battalions, you have to ask yourself what fine line divides Rallis's action against EAM from Zervas's. If I had the chance, I would kill Rallis stone dead, but I would prefer the opportunity to shoot the ELAS commanders, beginning with Aris and Saraphis.'

I am not justifying these attitudes; I merely inform you that they exist and that, rightly or wrongly, HMG is held to blame for the growth and present strength of EAM/ELAS. Yet at the same time the belief is widespread that only we can slay the dragon and it is confidently predicted that we shall be forced to do so in our own interest. Quoting Papandreou's truthful statement that EAM/ELAS has imposed an occupation on free Greece more terrible than that of the Wehrmacht, the question is put: How in the end will our measures and methods differ from those which are at present being employed against EAM, so that after liberation a democratic Government may be genuinely elected by the people and not fraudulently imposed by the 'people's representatives'? This is the heart of the matter. If this report is to be written off as another piece of prejudice, I ask you at least to preserve it and read it again in August 1945. By then, if not long before, we will see who was right.

The Greek office never commented on this report and I did not press for their reaction. It seemed wiser to bide my time and wait on events to justify my assessment, since we all knew that liberation was almost within our grasp.

Meantime, in spite of the curfew in Ioannina, the flow of information continued to reach us quite regularly. One particularly revealing item came from the Cherub team. It was the latest situation report dated 7 August 1944, prepared for Lanz by his Chief of Staff, which we summarized in a signal to Cairo ten days later. Lanz had been presented with the following assessment:

In early June and under pressure from the British, Zervas abandoned his up to now loyal attitude and attacked various guard posts, camps and columns on the Ioannina, Igoumenitsa, Arta and Preveza roads. After a few days, however, he stopped his operations and now keeps a neutral attitude, not giving in to Allied requests to resume his attacks on German troops. The recent imports of arms and supplies gave Zervas the opportunity to increase his strength by recruiting and organising new regiments. Now he has more than four divisions of 2-3 regiments each, 2 independent brigades and many independent formations, making a total strength of 20,000 men.[11] His units are well equipped with artillery, mortars and light machine guns.

At present, the allied liaison officers play their main role at Zervas's headquarters. The increased influence of the Allied Military Mission is undisputed especially in the Zervas area where such influence has led to his personal isolation during the operations which were carried out in early July. There seems to be some tension in Zervas's relations with the Allied Military Mission which should be attributed to his reversion to his loyal attitude towards the Germans and also to the resumption of his operations against the Communist bands. The relations of the Allied Military Mission with the Greek Communist bands have been strained for a long time. From prisoners' statements and from other reliable sources, we have come to the conclusion that for the time being there can be no question of British influence on the main ELAS Commanders. The activities of Allied Liaison Officers are solely limited to observation tasks, propaganda, espionage and sabotage against the Germans. The tension in such relations is attributable to the negative attitude of the Communist Commanders to the Papandreou Government and to the closer contact with Tito and the recent arrival of the Soviet mission at GHQ ELAS.[12] We must, however, reckon with the fact that the Allied Military Mission will continue its efforts to settle the controversies between Zervas and the Communists and also obtain recognition of the

[11] The true figure was somewhat over 10,000.
[12] This mission, headed by Colonel Popov, arrived on 25 July.

Papandreou Government by the Communists. It will be of primary importance if the Allies succeed in forcing Zervas to abandon for ever his up to now loyal attitude and if they can make use of his troops again for operations against the Germans. We must also reckon on the constant activity of Greek Communist bands in the whole area of XXII Mountain Corps if they are not checked by frequent drives or kept busy by attacks of EDES units.

This was the first time I had seen an official German document formally referring to Zervas's 'loyal attitude' and it both puzzled and disturbed me. My earlier suspicions that there had been some form of collusion at some level were now, as it were, confirmed in writing. My immediate reaction was to hurry over to Derviziana to discuss the implications of this discovery with Barnes, especially as I received a report from Kalousis just before leaving with the following relevant information: On 6 August Colonel Tarsakopoulos, the head of the Greek gendarmerie in Ioannina, had visited Zervas as an unofficial German intermediary to discuss further proposals for a truce between EDES and the Germans, designed to enable EDES to take over Ioannina on the German withdrawal and thereby prevent its seizure by EAM/ELAS. Zervas had spurned this offer, claiming that only GHQ and the Greek government in Cairo could take decisions on matters of such importance. Tarsakopoulos had immediately reported Zervas's negative reply to Tsimbris, the Governor of Ioannina, who had received similar approaches from the Germans. Both were considering going back to Zervas a second time to try and persuade him not to reject this unique opportunity of the 'free' capture of Ioannina. On 13 August, they had organized a public meeting in the Orpheus cinema in Ioannina during which they made vitriolic attacks on the ideology of EAM/ELAS.

On this occasion, Barnes agreed without hesitation that we should both see Zervas. But this time, without being able to explain it to myself, I sensed a certain embarrassment in Barnes's reaction to my information. He dismissed the reference to Zervas's 'loyal attitude' as 'the kind of rubbish we can expect from the Germans', but he did not question me as closely as I had expected about the activities of Tarsakopoulos and Tsimbris, brushing them aside as persons of minor importance. At the time,

I thought no more about it. In retrospect, and in the light of documents made available in the Public Record Office[13] and from Zervas's private diary,[14] it is clear why Barnes was somewhat ill at ease during our discussion. The explanation was that he had himself received a visit from Captain Michalakis, Lanz's Greek emissary on 4 August, who brought the following message. Just before the Wehrmacht attempt to overthrow Hitler (on 20 July 1944) the dissident generals had sent instructions to Lanz to arrange a meeting with Barnes, but during the delay necessary in finding and despatching the emissary it became obvious that the revolt had failed. Because Lanz had received no further instructions from the dissident group in Germany, he was now unable to meet Barnes 'officially'. But he still wished to arrange an 'unofficial' meeting on order to prepare the way for the re-occurrence of similar events.

Barnes replied that it was improbable that Cairo would agree to a meeting, but that he might arrange to meet Lanz 'unofficially'. Cairo's response to Barnes's report of this approach was a warning to proceed with the greatest caution and not exclude the possibility of a German effort 'to find out our future intentions, or to drive a wedge between ourselves and our Allies, or to discredit us or EDES in the eyes of the Greeks'. He was further instructed to avoid direct contact until he had established the bona fides of the emissary and clarified the situation. On 10 August Barnes had a second visit from Captain Michalakis, who said that Lanz 'accepted his proposals and was most willing to have a meeting. Unfortunately, he had been called to a conference in Salonica the same day and he suggested the meeting should be held on his return.' Barnes reported this to Cairo on 11 August and 'asked for the scope and subject of the talks so as to be able to act with more authority during the discussions'. In fact, there was no follow through to these approaches which, from the German viewpoint, were seen within the context of the political feelers that were put out at the same time through the Greek government in Athens. By 2 September Barnes had received instructions 'that GHQ was only interested in surrender', and Zervas's diary shows that on 9

[13] PRO: W. O. 201 1598; and in an article by Lars Baerentzen in *Scandinavian Studies in Modern Greek*, 4, 1980.
[14] Zervas's unpublished diary, p. 433.

September he told Michalakis that Lanz should stop bargaining about the terms of his surrender.

Before we went to meet Zervas, Barnes did not tell me a word about the two meetings he had had with Michalakis on 4 and 10 August, nor about the subsequent instructions he had received from Cairo. There was no reason why he should have done so, given his superiority to me in rank and the fact that he and I were representing two different and mutually uncooperative organizations in Cairo. It is quite likely that he was under orders to be tight-lipped. What is more surprising is the fact that no one in SOE briefed Woodhouse, who was in London at the time, about the negotiations; nor were they mentioned to him on his return either at Caserta or in Cairo or by Barnes when Woodhouse re-entered Greece in September. Moreover, the Greek office was probably ignorant of what had transpired between Barnes and Michalakis. In any event, I was not told anything about these matters. Captain Michalakis had recently come to my notice, however, from reports by both Kalousis and the Cherub team, not as Lanz's intermediary, but as an agent of the Sicherheitsdienst (Security Service). I had been shown one of the military reports he had offered to Zervas giving numerous identifications and locations of German units, which I knew to be false. In reporting this to the Greek office, I had added: 'Barnes informed.'

The meeting between Zervas, Barnes and myself had an unexpected outcome. As I was proceeding with my slow and overcarefully prepared introduction to the Tarsakopoulos affair – without, of course, mentioning the German document that referred to Zervas's 'up to now loyal attitude' – Zervas broke the tension with a burst of boyish laughter. He claimed he knew exactly what was cooking in Ioannina. When his laughter had subsided, he gave us his assurance that his reply to Lanz had been, and would continue to be, the blunt statement that any proposition from the German side could only be answered by GHQ and the Greek government in Cairo. In the event, Zervas kept his word and Tarsakopoulos returned to Ioannina with empty hands. This was quickly confirmed to me by Kalousis and other sources from Ioannina and I was therefore able to report the whole episode to the Greek office. As proof that Zervas did not use this occasion to parley with Lanz, he stepped up his harassing operations and a further trail of prisoners and deserters was sent to Tseritsana for interrogation.

In one operation near Menina, Zervas seized the opportunity to take reprisals on a number of Turco-Albanian villages which had formed a reliable Italian fifth column during the Greek-Albanian war in 1940-1 and had continued to cooperate with the Germans when they occupied Epirus. Their leader, Nuri Dino Bey, who lived in Ioannina, had been one of the most flagrant collaborators with the German intelligence services, whose activities we had followed and reported on for the past six months. Two junior German officers captured during this operation said they had been astonished when they were attacked by EDES units, as they had been assured that Lanz had successfully organized a truce with Zervas preparatory to the withdrawal of XXII Corps from western Greece. But by this time virtually all their information seemed of academic interest, since it became increasingly obvious that we were gathering detailed military intelligence on troops that would be well on their way home by the time Greece was finally liberated. Maniakis and I had such a mass of information from our own agent networks in Ioannina, Preveza and Arta, from prisoners and captured documents that our two wireless operators were unable to report it all.

We could now see clearly that the German appreciation was still to count on what they reckoned would be an inevitable second round of civil war between EDES and ELAS. One extract of a report to Lanz read:

Direct invasion of Greece cannot with reason be part of Allied strategy. Allied entry into Greece in its present condition will so quickly accelerate the existing political confusion that their military gains will be nullified. Even if we are forced to evacuate, Allied troops will probably be held back to await a fait accompli by one side or the other in a civil war which will be fought under the supervision of the British missions to both sides.

This was part of a much longer signal I sent to the Greek office, on which there was, as usual, no comment.

On 26 August we had firm information from the Cherub group in Ioannina that Lanz had finally given up hope of securing a truce with Zervas and saw no distinction between EDES and ELAS. Although he could not understand why Zervas had scorned his 'honourable offer', Lanz agreed with his Chief of Staff, in a conversation monitored by his interpreter and quickly reported to us, that it was only realistic for him to treat both EDES and ELAS as equal enemies. Zervas was visibly pleased when I reported this information to him in person. He said he intended to maintain his pressure on Lanz and he was as good as his word. The evidence that the tables were being turned was shown in my report on 3 September that the Germans were carrying out exercises for the defence of Ioannina against what they believed was the likelihood of Zervas's attack.

On 4 September XXII Corps headquarters and the Abwehr (Military Intelligence) and Sicherheitsdienst organizations began burning their papers and the Military Accounts branch closed its books. The following day Lanz flew to Athens to receive new orders. All this news reached us as fast as the couriers could walk from Ioannina to Tseritsana, and on 10 September I was able to signal that the end was now in sight. On his return from Athens Lanz announced to his staff that he had been authorized to negotiate the surrender of XXII Corps, if need be, to a regular army. But under no circumstances would he hand over to either EDES or ELAS. In other words, he would continue to fight them both until Allied troops arrived. At the same time he offended the Governor of Ioannina and the head of the gendarmerie (but not Zervas) by taking hostages as reprisals against EDES's attacks. On 8 September Lanz made a vigorous speech to all officers and NCO's at his headquarters, saying that they would fight to the last against the Russians and all *andartes*. But, significantly, he made no mention of what he intended to do in the event of an Allied landing. To his interpreter, however, he confirmed that he would surrender.

These were the best of times to be in mountain Greece. We were edging toward victory and eveyone wished to be in on the kill. New arrivals in Epirus, who brought news and gossip from London and Cairo, put me back in touch with the life I had left behind me and from which I had been artificially isolated during the past eight months. The first surprise visitor I received was David Wallace, who appeared in Tseritsana in mid August 1944 without warning and announced that he had been encouraged to come and talk to me by both Zervas and Barnes. I knew of him by name and reputation from the prominent part he had played in bringing the *andarte* delegation to Cairo a year before, in August 1943. But I did not know until he told me that on this as on his previous entry into mountain Greece, he was acting as Eden's personal representative and would be reporting his findings and assessments to him through Rex Leeper, with whose Embassy to the Greek government in exile in Cairo he had been in close touch during July. We became friends in five minutes and he relieved me of all embarrassment by calling me Nigel straightaway and laughing my pseudonym to scorn. He was an undergraduate generation senior to me at Oxford where we had never met; but we found in a flash that we shared a handful of the same friends at Balliol and knew many of the same dons. Indeed, it was Tom Boase who had told him to look me up – and who much later published the notes Wallace had prepared before the war in his research on Frankish castles in Greece. It was then, and later while serving as Press Attaché at the British Embassy in Athens from September 1939 until the German invasion in April 1941, that he acquired a fluent knowledge of the language and an understanding of Greek politics. Over the first two cups of coffee, I naturally brought myself up to date with what had happened to mutual friends: who had been killed or captured or decorated or disgraced or married or covered in scandal. This could have gone on much longer, such was my thirst for news, and my excitement at the first chance of a rich gossip about people, so reminiscent of prewar Oxford. But a sense of discipline asserted itself and we agreed to talk shop. We did nothing else for the next two days.

I plunged in at the deep end and showed him a copy of the most recent political report I had sent out by safe hand on 10 August and was greatly relieved to find him substantially in agreement with it, especially with the answers to the questions that had been put to me on the organization and objectives of EAM/ELAS. I also showed him my earlier political reports and was scarcely surprised to learn that he had not seen them either in the Foreign Office or in the British Embassy in Cairo. We had a healthy exchange of views about the hostile relationship between SIS and SOE in Cairo, but Wallace was the first person to enlighten me on the quite different reputation and standing of SIS in Whitehall.

We also spoke very frankly to one another about the qualifications required for someone holding Tom Barnes's position as head of the Allied Military Mission in Epirus. We agreed that his qualities as a brilliant sapper and sabotage expert, as well as being a natural leader of men, especially if they were guerrillas, had been more than amply demonstrated since the destruction of the Gorgopotamos viaduct in November 1942. But who could have foreseen that in the aftermath of that event political rather than technical or standard military qualifications were what would be required of those who remained to organize the Greek resistance? We agreed that Woodhouse in Thessaly was the shining but rare example of someone who had a sophisticated understanding of the political requirements of his mission. He had no equivalent in Epirus, where only a few British officers were equipped to handle political assignments.

Wallace explained to me that he had spent the early part of August touring the EDES 3rd Division area, which covered the whole of Zervas-held territory east of the Ioannina-Arta road and was commanded by Lieutenant Colonel Papathanassiou (an incessant talker, who never drew breath) from his headquarters in Plaisia where I had landed the previous December. Wallace had been struck by the fact that most of this Division had been locked up in the same positions monitoring the movements of their ELAS compatriots across the frontier since the Plaka armistice in February. Here was a classic example of the Germans profiting from being the second enemy. Much more could and should have been done to harass the Germans on the Ioannina-Arta and Ioannina-Metsovo roads, but virtually all the officers of the 3rd Division considered that their prime purpose was to stand ready to fight ELAS, which was continually probing the territory held by Zervas.

After reading and commenting on my political reports, Wallace showed me a copy of the detailed analysis he had made of the EDES organization on 30 July, which had been despatched to Leeper by safe hand in mid August shortly before he left Zervas's headquarters at Derviziana.[15] I copied out and made a précis of

[15] See J. M. Stevens, C. M. Woodhouse and D. J. Wallace, *British Reports on Greece 1943-44*, edited by Lars Baerentzen (Museum Tusculanum Press, Copenhagen, 1982), pp. 119-59.

what seemed to me the main points, many (but not all) of which compared closely with my appreciation. In his introduction Wallace looked back to the start of the civil war (the First Round) in October 1943, and recalled how advantage had been taken of Eden's presence in Cairo at the time to lift the ban imposed by GHQ on the supply of arms to either side in favour of Zervas, on the two grounds that he was obviously not the aggressor and that he was a valuable and reliable ally of HMG. 'Since that time,' he wrote,

in spite of occasional debates in Cairo and of considerable variations in the actual execution, our policy has in fact been the unilateral supply of Zervas. On the other hand, at a certain moment during the civil war Zervas was anxious to get out of the narrow area into which he had been pressed between ELAS and the Germans and to undertake a major counter-offensive into ELAS territory. He was, however, forbidden to do any such thing and was ordered to remain on the defensive, avoiding any provocative action that might cause an extension of the civil war. To this day, Zervas likes to think that but for this order he would have marched into Thessaly and would have been welcomed by an enthusiastic population and EAM/ELAS would have been no more. My view on this, after discussing it with Lt Colonels Hammond, Barnes and Torrance is that Zervas would in fact and in time have been totally liquidated, leaving ELAS the only armed body of Greeks in the country. It therefore follows that, however spontaneous the movement may have been at the beginning and however much support it may now enjoy, Zervas is a British creation in the sense that we are responsible for his continued existence and for all the consequences that may follow therefrom. He has been a completely loyal ally and will still do exactly what we tell him. He is therefore not only our creation, but remains an instrument in our hands. He now has an organised force of over 10,000 men who are better armed, better equipped and have a higher morale than the numerically larger, though more scattered forces of ELAS. He could extend his frontiers at the expense of ELAS and he could compel the Germans to evacuate Western Greece, unless they were able and willing to increase their forces. He now controls a strip of coast and is being supplied by sea on a scale far beyond anything previously attempted in Greece. It is only our policy that limits the rate at which this supply should be maintained or extended. He holds a beachhead and an area in which Allied troops might be landed any time we wished or in which the Royal Greek government would be able, if need be when the time comes, to set itself up in Greece. Zervas has in fact long ceased to be a liability; he has become an asset and is capable of being a major factor in any general policy we wish to pursue in Greece.

HMG's policy was made clear in the Foreign Secretary's statement in the House of Commons on 27 July.[16] We wish to see the unity of all Greeks, including EAM, against the Germans. If unity proves unobtainable, we are clearly committed without any further havering to full support of the Greek Government and to not wishing at any cost to see EAM establish themselves in Greece. Now that we have taken this open political stand against them, it must follow that even militarily we can expect ever decreasing military cooperation from ELAS, who have always regarded Operation Noah's Ark[17] as a British interest and who are scarcely likely to continue to regard Britain as a friend or even as much worth conciliating. It therefore follows that militarily also we should be wise to attach increased importance to Zervas and the opportunities his position offers for development . . .

At the moment, the indications are that ELAS definitely intends to try for the seizure of the monopoly of power. They have denounced Papandreou as well as Zervas as traitors. They are probing the strength of Zervas's forces all along the line. They are massacring their political opponents wherever they can lay their hands on them, in Athens, any towns they can enter and in the villages. Unless Allied troops arrive in the country to take over the main centres from the Germans, or we reinforce Zervas to a point where he can take offensive action to protect the population in territory at present controlled by ELAS, there will be a most bloody slaughter ending in a Communist dictatorship . . .

Zervas still remains slightly suspicious of GHQ in Cairo, though the scale on which he has recently been supplied has made him for the first time almost confident of their attitude towards him; he had not however forgotten Brigadier Keble's[18] reply to his appeals for help in October 1943, when he was within an ace of being crushed between ELAS and the 1st Mountain Division. He was then told that arms were supplied by the British to fight the Germans and not for civil war: a statement unimpeachable in itself but irritating in the circumstances. He certainly feels the greatest confidence in and friendship for Tom Barnes, combined with a healthy respect owing to the firmness with which the latter treats him when in a fractious mood. Both Barnes and Torrance refuse to allow him to embroil them in political debates and keep their co-operation on a purely military basis, operational and administrative.

His attitude on being informed of the arrival of the Russian Military

[16] Its gist was HMG's regret that EAM had declined to ratify the decisions of their representatives at the Lebanon conference in May or to appoint ministers to the posts in Papandreou's Government of National Unity in Cairo, which it was agreed should be reserved for them. In fact they joined on 15 August. The proximity of this date to 25 July when Colonel Popov's Russian Military Mission to ELAS arrived without warning, fostered the belief that EAM was acting on Soviet advice.
[17] The plan to harass the German withdrawal.
[18] Chief of Staff, SOE, Cairo.

125

Mission at ELAS headquarters at the end of July was simply that we might be surprised, but he certainly was not. This only confirmed his view that we should soon find ourselves faced in the Balkans with a bloc including Tito, the Albanian and Bulgarian communists, and EAM, all under Russian influence and receiving Russian support. He hoped we knew how we should deal with this problem. He saw no evidence of it so far. He did not know what our policy was. Perhaps that was what we wanted. Certainly there was little he could do about it alone . . .

Inside EDES controlled territory, its organisation has improved vastly since 1943. If it had not, Zervas would not indeed be able to maintain a force of just over 10,000 men, mostly well equipped and with a full complement of arms. There is now a telephone network to all units and to any villages of importance; it works and is much used by the Allied Mission, though at some cost to their tempers and to what is left of their philhellenism. The distribution of stores landed from the sea operations is a colossal task and imposes a heavy strain on the limited transport facilities. Huge convoys of mules are gathered from all over the country many days in advance. The efficiency with which the boats are unloaded, at an average rate of one ton per minute, apparently astounded the Royal Navy. All the doctors in the area are now considered mobilised, paid a fixed salary and sent where they are wanted to attend either military or civilian patients without fee.

The Press and Propaganda Services are doing their job fairly well . . . Daily bulletins from the BBC are issued and Greek news, e.g. Papandreou's speeches and the Lebanon Conference, is circulating here in type and generally known within a week of being broadcast . . . During the Greek news broadcasts the telephone is held close to the loudspeaker and quite a number of units and districts get their news rapidly by this means. I am also assured that news and propaganda material is regularly smuggled across the border into ELAS territory. This source of news is of course supplemented by a greater volume coming up from the German occupied towns in the area. I have questioned several people from Thessaly who confirm that the important news does get around, ELAS being able only to hinder not to prevent it . . .

There are the usual jealousies and frictions between the EDES commanders who include both Royalists and Venezelists, but Zervas has succeeded in making them both lie down together and in preventing political issues from dividing his forces: which is more than the Greek Government in Cairo has ever done.

It would be hard to estimate where the King's stock stands in this area, as no one ever mentions his name. I have heard it said that if Zervas came out in open support of the King, he would swing almost everyone behind him. There is no sign of any hostility such as I remarked last year . . .

Royalist officers have served him better than the Venizelists. I suspect that he is even coming round to the monarch in his own heart; certainly he showed me with immense pride a crucifix, given to him by Prince Paul and Princess Frederica and engraved with their initials which had been brought back to him from Cairo after the Lebanon Conference . . . At the second anniversary of Zervas's flight from Athens on 23 July 1942, there was an impressive parade and a memorial to the Unknown Andarte of EDES was unveiled by Zervas. The Bishop of Paramythia celebrated mass which was followed by an impressive parade of 1,200 armed andartes who marched past the memorial in good order. There was a great feast with huge quantities of food and drink followed by traditional Greek dances. Representatives from all the villages in the area came and laid wreaths. For a time, Zervas sat under a tree, like St Louis, and heard grievances and claims from anyone who wished. Some 2,000 rounds of live ammunition were discharged during the day, which is less than usual, and there was only one brawl which was rapidly quelled. It was noticeable that the speeches and the andarte songs were all largely directed against EAM and there was a certain amount of shouting 'Let us march into Thessaly'. The liturgy included in the mass featured a request that the Lord might have mercy on his faithful servant Napoleon Zervas, but there was no mention of the King.

After passing some unfavourable remarks about certain members of Pyromaglou's political bureau and the shady reputations of some of EDES's military commanders – apart from the notable exception of Major Agoros, who commanded the crack EDES 3/40 Regiment and was always sent wherever the battle was thickest – Wallace's report finished with some comments on EAM/ELAS. Quoting his last conversation with Lieutenant Colonel Hammond, who had recently been visiting Epirus from ELAS territory, he said that the Political Committee of National Liberation (PEEA), the shadow government which EAM/ELAS had set up in March, was run by the hardliners Siantos and Ioannides.

It was obvious that the personnel of the liberal façade were quite without influence and virtually prisoners . . . Everyone in ELAS territory knew what the situation was, and the Liberal delegates in Cairo were probably right in saying that their resignation from the Committee would not be effective there. Probably their main preoccupation was the presence of some of their families and a certain number of their adherents in the mountains. Reprisals would certainly have been taken against them. The stock of Saraphis, never very high, had fallen noticeably since his return from Cairo, and Despotopoulos[19] was now publicly rude to him. In Hammond's opinion, the best time for engineering a split in EAM/ELAS had passed, as their hold over the towns accessible to their area was now so strong that there was nowhere for dissidents to take refuge or establish themselves. There was little to be said for a policy of open denunciation of ELAS and withdrawal of the British Mission. Everyone now knew that we were not supplying ELAS so they got no prestige from our support. Such action would in fact remove the last brake on ELAS terrorism and would be followed by an orgy of murder and pillage, for which the population would blame us, while the Allied Mission personnel would certainly be exposed to violence by the irresponsible hooligan elements of ELAS. In fact, ELAS was impressed with Zervas's present strength and an all out offensive against him was not at this juncture likely. Their interest had in consequence been largely diverted to the towns and it was certain that as soon as the Germans left, their first objective would be to seize power in the towns and massacre all their political opponents. Unless Allied troops came in, it was by no means certain that they would not succeed in establishing an armed dominion over the whole country. They would have no difficulty in seizing all the towns between Athens and Salonica . . . The resources of Epirus were not sufficient for Zervas successfully to oppose this in the long run unless we intervened to assist him. Athens was of course the key to the situation, but there again ELAS had a considerable force inside and there would be nothing to prevent them sending reinforcements from the mountains. It was in fact essential that we should send in troops . . .

Wallace's report on his tour of the EDES 3rd Division area ended with the gloomy reflection that 'our effort in Greece, in men and money, has not only been out of all proportion to the results we have achieved against the Germans, but also to the value of the Greek people, who are not capable of being saved from themselves, nor for themselves worth it. This is also the unanimous opinion of all British liaison officers, who have been long in the country.' When Wallace said that he assumed I subscribed to this view, I replied that I most definitely did not do so. I said that I completely understood the exasperation of most SOE officers, who were profoundly uninterested in the political affiliations of foreigners, in finding themselves embroiled day and night in passionate political arguments with individuals whose natural disposition was to disagree with one another and find

[19] A member of the *andarte* delegation to Cairo in 1943.

consensus almost unnatural. You either felt warmly attached to, and fascinated by the political habits of the eastern Mediterranean, or you found the whole thing both absurd and obnoxious. I considered myself lucky to be in the former category.

This was the only point on which we differed. On all other matters of political evaluation, we found ourselves in close agreement. Perhaps the most valuable aspect of our lengthy talks was the opportunity it gave me to learn at first hand from such a well-placed witness of the suspicion and mistrust of SOE which was shared by both the Foreign Office and Rex Leeper's Embassy in Cairo. It was from Wallace that I heard of Churchill's violent hostility to Myers after 1943 and of the slow progress that Leeper had made in grasping the significance of the constitutional issue. He also confirmed to me what I had long suspected, that SIS, in both London and Cairo, had no more than a walk-on part to play in the Greek drama. Above all, we were completely in focus on the most important issue at that juncture: which was not to debate whether EAM/ELAS would make a bid for power, but to try to discover when and how the attempt would be made. Wallace finally assured me that after his short mission was completed and he returned to Cairo, he would personally take up with Leeper and the head of ISLD in Cairo the question of what had happened to my political reports. He said that in no circumstances would he allow my last report of 10 August, which we had discussed at such length, to be suppressed in either Cairo or London. In any event, he would see the head of the Greek office and demand a full explanation. In fact, he was never able to do any of these things. At the end of his stay he left Tseritsana to observe an operation which EDES was planning against the Germans at Menina near Paramythia, and was killed at the start of the skirmish on 19 August. Our two-day friendship, on which I had counted so much, thus came to a sad and sudden end.

Others with whom I came in touch during August were Ian Scott-Kilvert and Arthur Foss, who had recently arrived and represented the Political Warfare Bureau in Cairo. Once again my Jim Russell pseudonym did not work as I had met Ian Scott-Kilvert in Cambridge before the war and in his case too we shared a number of friends. So this made for a good start to a short but close collaboration with both of them in designing their prop-

aganda leaflets, which our agent networks distributed in Ioannina, Preveza, Arta and Agrinion. In this way much of the local
intelligence we had gathered throughout the summer and which I
had not considered worth reporting to Cairo was in the end put to
good practical use. Bit by bit, I felt myself becoming a more
normal person as I slowly regained contact with my previous life.

Another visitor who helped me forward in this direction was
Costas Achillopoulos. He knocked at my door one day in late
August, believing (wrongly) that I could provide him with a bath,
and introduced himself as a 'Free French photo reporter'. I took
to him immediately and, as with David Wallace, lapped up
eagerly all the news he brought from London and Cairo, as I soon
discovered that we knew many of the same people. Our
friendship quickly developed as he stayed in my house for the
next two weeks, fascinating the small world of Tseritsana with
his gaiety and style and the happy mixture of French, Greek and
English that flavoured his conversation. The attractive combina-
tion of his technical equipment (a camera and a paint box) and his
habit of sunbathing outside my house made him the kind of
personality – so splendidly different from all the British officers –
that the village had never seen before. His fame as a photographer
increased after the war. A sketch of the church in Tseritsana,
which he gave me as a leaving present, has remained with me as a
treasured possession and a token of our long friendship.

In mid September the Germans made a drive to open the
Ioannina-Preveza road in order to evacuate their troops from the
coast. We knew this was their objective and had received ample
warning of the operation which brought them close to Tseritsana.
As a precaution, we were all packed and ready to move in case
they came through to burn the village as a final act of retaliation,
but in the event we watched their patrols pass us by. This was my
last sight of them.

On 19 September I signalled that XXII Corps in Ioannina was
beginning to be disbanded and that German columns were
heading for Koritsa in Albania, after negotiating with the
opposing factions of the Tseta and the Balli Kombetar what
proved to be an unimpeded passage through Albania. On the
same day, immediately after the German evacuation, fighting

broke out in Agrinion between EAM and the Security Battalions. But our information from Ioannina repeated that if Allied paratroops landed in the Ioannina plain, Lanz was still ready to surrender. By 22 September the Germans had pulled out of both Missolonghi and Preveza and Lanz flew to Corfu to supervise the removal of his last remaining troops. By 25 September EDES had occupied Arta and Igoumenitsa; the only Germans left in Epirus were grouped in Ioannina, Metsovo and Konitsa.

Papandreou's government had in the meantime moved from Cairo to Salerno, Italy on 7 September after six representatives on EAM had agreed to join his Government of National Unity on 2 September. In late September Zervas and Saraphis were invited to General Wilson's headquarters at Caserta to meet Lieutenant General Ronald Scobie, who had been appointed General Officer Commanding the British Forces destined for Greece, and Harold Macmillan, Minister Resident at Allied HQ. Zervas took Pyromaglou with him, but Saraphis's role as the commander of ELAS was overshadowed by John Zevgos, who was one of the Communist ministers in Papandreou's government. On 26 September both EDES and ELAS signed the Caserta agreement by which all the guerrilla forces operating in Greece placed themselves under the orders of the Greek Government of National Unity, which in turn put them under Scobie's command. ELAS and EDES agreed to harass the German withdrawal in the territories they controlled; as regards Athens, it was agreed that no action would be taken except under Scobie's direct orders. Papandreou had rightly argued that if EAM were not included in his government, ELAS would take over Athens directly after the Germans left and before the Greek government or Scobie's forces could arrive.

It was scarcely surprising that in this situation all our sources of information pelted us with protests against the absence of Allied troops. The situation was made worse by the fact that the official Greek broadcasts on the BBC, which had a particularly eager and attentive audience, were taking a favourable line towards EAM and, worse still, to Bulgaria. I tried to reflect this growing uneasiness in my report of 26 September:

From Ioannina, Arta and Preveza, we now hear that the following questions are being asked with bitterness: Where is the famous Allied support and Anglo-American interest in the future of Greece? Is our future at Russia's disposal because the Anglo-Americans are too weak politically or militarily to send troops? Now that Preveza, Missolonghi and Parga are open, is not the fact that no landing has taken place proof that the Anglo-Americans have lost interest or cannot afford to take an interest in Greece? The civilian population in the liberated towns cannot understand why Allied troops are not already in Epirus and why there is such a startling lack of any form of Allied initiative. When the BBC announces that there is a British Military Mission in Sofia, the first reaction here is to ask why there had been no official statement about Macedonia by Papandreou on the BBC, which allows the Bulgarian Prime Minister to air his views. This has naturally given rise to rumours that HMG is trampling on Papandreou and that some deal is being fixed up with the Russians, which will result in Greek interests being sold down the river. Such rumours take better shape when viewed against the oddity of some of the broadcasts from London. Why was the BBC more than ten days behind the times in reporting the presence of EDES in Preveza and Levkas, while they had given EAM the benefit of occupying Konitsa, which is in fact still held by the Germans? You should also know that propaganda leaflets, printed in Thessaly and signed by the Communist Party (KKE) have in the last few days been circulating in Ioannina for the first time. They call for a fighting alliance and national union under EAM-ELAS against the Germans and the 'Gestapo-Edesites'. Thus we are witnessing the opening rounds of the next stage of civil war.

On 26 September Lanz took his final panic measures before evacuating Ioannina and allowed indiscriminate shooting and arrests. We heard that Kalousis had gone to ground and I sent his courier back with a message that his first duty was to stay alive and uncaptured. The following day Tsombos and his team arrived in Tseritsana after narrowly escaping Lanz's roundup. They had warning that all three of them were on his list and were likely to be shot if found. So they wisely decided to leave within minutes of receiving this vital tip-off, which came from a Greek agent working for the Sicherheitsdienst, who for several months past had kept Tsombos regularly informed of German espionage activities. As a final service he threw in for good measure the code name Cherub, which I had used in all my signals for reporting this team's information since their recruitment in January. In addition, he told Tsombos that 'Blue Eyes and Jupiter had better get out of Ioannina as soon as possible'. Such was their relief to have escaped Lanz's clutches that Tsombos and his team tossed this information over to me with the merry comment that their friend in the Sicherheitsdienst appeared to be suffering from hallucinations.

My reaction, which I had to conceal from them both then and thereafter, was the polar opposite of theirs. If the Sicherheitsdienst knew the identities and code names of Tsombos and his collaborators (Cherub), of Kalousis (Blue Eyes) and one of his subsources (Jupiter), it was unmistakably obvious that my codes had been broken and all my wireless traffic had been read by the Germans since January. Furthermore, since my simple letter transposition code was based, as I well knew, on exactly the same system as was used by the Allied Military Mission at Derviziana, it seemed reasonable to assume that all Barnes's wireless traffic had given the German cryptographers no more of a problem than mine. So our growing satisfaction throughout 1944 that we had been able to follow with proven accuracy what was happening in most of the area controlled by XXII Corps had presumably been matched by Lanz's knowledge of our performance and activities. He knew about us what we knew about him – not to mention his presumed coverage of SOE's wireless traffic from Zervas's headquarters at Derviziana. My first thought, however,was for Kalousis, who was clearly in danger, though I could not reveal this unhappy fact to anyone around me. All I could do was cross my fingers and touch wood that he was successfully planning his escape.

That evening was not, however, spent reflecting on these mysteries, which seemed academic when we knew that the Germans would so soon be out of sight. This was a time for celebration and half the village came to join us. In mid September I had had a generous drop of supplies from Bari and there were tins of food stacked in a corner of my little house. Four bottles of whisky had also been included in the drop. So we were well equipped to receive our friends and a party was quickly prepared. We sang and danced until there was no further strength within us. We behaved as if the war were won. I remember, too, the particular beauty of that night, when it seemed that a million extra stars appeared. I had drunk more than my fill with the rest of them. But when they collapsed with fatigue and flopped down to sleep on the floor, on the stone paving outside the house or wherever there was space, I found myself with a second wind. Suddenly I felt reinvigorated, with no wish whatever to sleep. So I crept away on my own, went for a long walk and lay on my back to watch the glory of the sky until the start of dawn.

This must have been about the fiftieth time that I had looked up at the night and tried to work out what to make of this whole Greek experience. But on this occasion I was not thinking of the Germans or the political consequences of their withdrawal. I was not fretting about the Greek office, which seemed as far away and as irrelevant as Tokyo. I was not thinking how or when the war would end, nor what would happen to me thereafter. On this occasion I enjoyed one of those rare moments of pride that I had lived, worked, struggled and fought with the kind of people who had shared the evening's celebration. To have gone some way to being accepted as one of them – which was the way they put it – seemed to have made the whole of the adventure worth while. It was all too easy to put a critical apparatus to work on the leaders; but before these people, whose titles were not in their military ranks but in their Christian names, I could only bow my head. They had no great claims on life. They were not dreaming of marble halls and the glittering tinsel of victory. Their simple village lives had been disrupted by foreign invasions and their consequences. In response, they had given all that was best within them: their courage and instinctive guile, their refusal to submit, their intelligent and critical reserve about the motives of some of their leaders, their solidarity with their compatriots in Epirus and their readiness to sacrifice all they had in the cause of liberation. They had shown me, as a foreigner in their midst, a warmth and a hospitality that was explained, as I very well knew, not by my manners or appearance, but by what was represented in the uniform I wore. In the small communities of mountain Epirus, there was an unquestioned acceptance of the value of the British connection. This gave every officer the opportunity of deluding himself that he was in the direct line of descent from Byron. Flattery from any quarter is easy to assimilate, but what caused me some anxiety was their unshakeable confidence in the future. None of them doubted that the British connection would bring to

Greece guarantees of political stability, social justice and a better life. It was unthinkable that we would let them down. They were sure that good times were round the corner. On countless occasions I had heard it said: 'the British will find a solution.' How many times had I asked myself why there was such trust in us? But on that night pride glowed within me that I had had the chance of living this experience.

The following day, when I had sobered up and returned from romance to reality, I had to consider when and how to inform both Barnes and the Greek office that my codes certainly, and SOE's in all likelihood, had been broken. On reflection, I decided to wait awhile to see if there were any further developments, especially in the hope that Kalousis would be able to join us. I was also expecting that the Greek office might be able to shed some light on these matters, in view of a mysterious top priority signal I had received on 29 August. It read: 'Germans are in possession of a code which is stated to belong to No 41 W/T Set in Ioannina area and they are following exchange of messages. Can it be that one of your chaps had your code written and has lost it? If not, can you offer any solution? Reply quickly.' My immediate answer was as follows: 'What is connection between my mission and W/T Set 41? Sets used by Katsikakis and Mulholland have nothing to do with figures 41. None of our codes lost in the way you suggest. We are all mystified by whole affair. Was 41 W/T Set captured by Germans from SOE as part of Operation Steinadler's successful drive against ELAS and capture of Pendalofos in early July?' There was no response to this signal and my final question went unanswered. But at least I was aware from the end of August that Cairo had some means of monitoring German wireless traffic.

Mercifully, my main problem quickly solved itself. Kalousis managed to slip out of Ioannina and joined the rest of us in Tseritsana at the beginning of October. He arrived looking fresh as a daisy with the welcome news that none of his informers, who had worked so steadily for him throughout the year, had been arrested. This gave me the opportunity to make my last visit to Derviziana to tell Barnes and Zervas that my network of agents in Ioannina had suffered no casualties, and at the same time explain to them why I had 'gone off the air' after such clear evidence that my codes had been broken. When I put the point that their position might be similar to my own, they both thought that I was making much ado about nothing and Barnes laughingly commented that he had more important things to think about. He may well have been right. In any event, it was an understandable reaction in the circumstances, when everyone was packing up and preparing for the excitements of a new existence in the towns, which would be far removed in every sense from mountain life in Epirus. On my return from Derviziana I signalled the Greek office: 'For reasons which I most obviously cannot explain, I strongly suspect my codes have been bust by the Germans. Please therefore send me nothing compromising to yourselves in the future.'

During my last days in the village, while we were waiting for Lanz to leave, I had ample time to try to make a cool assessment for myself of what purposes, if any, had been achieved by my mission. My original instructions were to focus exclusively on reporting the German order of battle in western Greece. I knew that I had carried out these orders and had provided virtually all the information that was needed. Each questionnaire from GHQ had been answered in detail by the intelligence networks we had set up in the towns and by the close coverage of the traffic movements along all the main roads. Some important documentary evidence had been provided by our agents and even more had been handed over to us by prisoners and deserters. Without the help from all levels of EDES and from Barnes I could have got nowhere. With their help, which had been freely offered and not acquired by any skill on my part, the military targets had all been hit. As it turned out, this had been an easy assignment. Any fool could have done it.

Two things, however, marred my satisfaction on this score. The first was the fact that in the end it had proved to be an academic exercise. The Germans were leaving of their own accord; they would not be beaten in battles that our intelligence had helped to win. We had doubtless made the war map at GHQ in Cairo look more impressive with clusters of little flags identifying the strength, equipment and morale of the units on the mainland of western Greece and in the northern Ionian Islands. But the provision of this information had not altered Lanz's timetable and made him leave Greece sooner. Lanz himself confirmed this in 1950 when, writing of his experience, he put the contribution of the Greek resistance into its historical perspective:

In the summer of 1944 ... aside from Rumania's and Bulgaria's defection, which was furthered by the guerrillas and the subsequent advance on Belgrade, it was principally Tito's army of partisans that forced the Germans to evacuate the Balkans. This was the first occasion that an organised guerrilla organisation achieved a strategic victory.

The second source of disappointment was the evidence that my codes had been broken. This destroyed the myth of secrecy so cherished by everyone operating behind the enemy's lines. If we had provided an accurate record of the German positions and potential, they must have been aware of what we had been doing. This, of course, prompted the question in my mind why they had not acted on their information and tried to destroy the intelligence networks we had built up. Progressively throughout the year I had been aware of Lanz's hope that he could wean Zervas away from his tight links with the Allied Military Mission and thereby profit from full-scale civil war between ELAS and EDES. There had been periods in early summer, during the circumstantial semi-truce between Zervas and Lanz, which were explained by Cairo's instructions to both EDES and ELAS to lie low and hold their forces in reserve. At no time could Zervas relax his watch on ELAS. But it was not plain to me until I was confronted by the evidence how much my work had benefited from the political circumstances. At the time I could find no satisfactory explanation as to why Lanz had allowed our intelligence operations to go forward when he could so easily have arrested and broken up many of our network of Greek informers. In retrospect, this situation has not been much clarified. Even allowing for the fact that counter-intelligence services have a natural proclivity to watch and wait, once enemy intelligence agents have been identified, so as to widen the knowledge of their activities, it still does not explain why Lanz took no action just before the Germans withdrew from Ioannina. His wish to keep a line open to EDES until the last moment, which he might turn to advantage in contacting the British if it were possible to arrange a surrender to them and not to any *andarte* force, might explain why he did not act on his information sooner. But it does not account for his inaction after his ultimate disillusion with Zervas.

At least I was comforted that I had been right to devote a large part of my time to political analysis, because I innocently hoped that what I had reported might help to win the political battle which then seemed unavoidable after the German withdrawal. On this score I knew that what I had sent out to the Greek office did not tally with Barnes's uncritical evaluation of EDES and of Zervas in particular. How my information fitted in with the plethora of reports from other sources was, of course, unknown to me. For that reason, I was determined to get to Athens at the first available opportunity; only there could I discover from the Greek office, which had received my political reports in silence all the year, whether my mission had achieved its minimum political purpose. All I knew for certain from David Wallace was that he had not seen – either in the Foreign Office or in the British Embassy in Cairo – any of my reports analysing the extreme likelihood of an armed clash between EAM/ELAS and its opponents in the aftermath of the German evacuation.

What none of us knew at the time was that in May 1944 Eden had made a tentative proposal to the Soviet Ambassador in London suggesting an agreement whereby Rumanian affairs would be in the main the concern of the Soviet government, while Greek affairs would be in the main a British concern. In September the Soviet government confirmed this agreement about respective spheres of military operations in principle and declared that they had no objection to the despatch of British forces to Greece and no intention of sending Soviet forces into that country. Moreover, Stalin and Churchill, at a meeting in Moscow on 9 October 1944, had agreed to the relative influence of the great powers in the Balkan countries, as expressed in the following percentages: Rumania: Russia 90%/others 10%; Greece: Great Britain 90% (in accord with the U.S.)/Russia 10%; Hungary and Yugoslavia: 50/50%; Bulgaria: Russia 75%/others 25%. If indeed such a story had reached us, even in garbled form, it would have been waved away as rubbish in ELAS territory, where Stalin's lack of interest in Greece would have been incredible; and Zervas would probably have suspected that a

10% Soviet interest would have been enough to cause real trouble.

In my last days in Tseritsana, when everyone knew we were on the point of leaving, visitors came streaming in from the villages close by to bid farewell to Maniakis and myself and ask that they should be kept in touch with our news. Now that we were scattering to distant parts, it was as if the family was breaking up. It was only then that I realized that the excitement of liberation was tempered by a sadness that I was leaving behind me the warmth of a life I would never live again. Our visitors recalled a host of tiny incidents that I had forgotten. Do you remember, I was asked, the day you stopped with us on your way back from Derviziana when you were shivering with cold and sneezing every other minute, and then it all seemed to pass in a flash when we gave you a hot drink and the sun suddenly came out? You said that a winter sun like that did not exist in England. Don't you remember the day when Nikos and Aristides had a row over which was the stronger of his two mules and you said that if God had made you into a mule you would have been the worst one in the whole of Lakka Souli because the most you could do was carry a haversack on your back? Do you remember the party we had when we taught you to sing Greek songs? Do you remember the day when we told you Mr Mario must have found the girl he loved because he looked so happy and you pretended you knew nothing about it? Do you remember when Nikos got so drunk that he couldn't walk home to Tseritsana and we had to unload the stores you were bringing from Derviziana and put him on one of the mules, and when you came back to fetch them the next day, you left us two tins of sausages? We will never forget how worried you looked, and how cross you were, when your charging engine was broken and your batteries were not strong enough for your messages to go out to Cairo and we said: 'Never mind, they will send another one; it's not so serious.' Such reminiscences of tiny incidents showed how closely they had participated in our everyday life.

From Preveza, Arta and Parga we had joyful messages from our agents now that the Germans were gone, asking how they could keep in touch with us when we moved to Ioannina – and in particular, how long their payments would continue. Indeed

asking for favours, which had been a constant – and understandable – theme to which I had grown accustomed in the previous
nine months, culminated in my receiving the following poem
brought by hand from an unknown literary figure on the island of
Levkas. The heart of the matter was in the postscript. Written in
splendid English, it read:

From Mr Panos Catapodes – Vurnicas, Levkas (Santa Maura), Ionian
Islands, Greece
To Captain Jim – Somewhere in Greece

10th October, 1944

CAPTAIN JIM

Captain Jim, I greet you!
Wings of silent fame
Brought to me your name
Name of a British soldier on Grecian soil,
Who valourously for Liberty doth toil,

I would like to meet you
For to exchange a smile
And to chatter a while
With you as friends, and as sincere allies,
Immune of horrid diplomatic lies.

I too am a fighter,
Ever pressing forward:
Yet, not with the sword,
But, with a no less powerful arm
With the pen that could an host disarm.

Yes, I am a writer
And a song tune I
Live for Truth, or die!
Fight for Justice – not others to fleece
But he never dies who dies for *Greece*!

P.S.

I – A REQUEST

Of things by War denied to Greeks – and me!
I miss nothing so much as a cup of tea.
Tea does so much please, refresh, exhilarate
That helps to draw love thoughts even out of hate.

I am told that of tea you have big heaps
(All good things from all countries England sweeps!)
May I ask of you a very great favour
to send me please some tea with fine flavour?
That if you do for me, dear Captain Jim
I, in return will write for you a hymn!

II – MY CARD (FROM 'MY STORY')

I have been a Londoner for years –
Not as a merchant but as it appears
From this not unworthy, if simple rhyme,
With the muses, I whiled away my time . . .

Note: Captain Jim's name was first made known to the writer in 1943.

Alas, the hymn was never written, as tea was one of the few commodities I did not have: but I wrote him a gushing letter of thanks – in prose.

On the morning of 15 October 1944 Lanz himself led the last convoy out of Ioannina. As the evidence from the Nuremberg trials shows, his final act of independence was to disobey the orders of Army Group E in Salonica to destroy all stores and supplies and leave the earth scorched before evacuation. There was no destruction of civilian installations. In an earlier demonstration of his anti-Nazi views, Lanz had refused to provide shipping space for the deportation of Jews from Corfu in June 1944. But these were the retrospective qualities of a German general, who was critical of Hitler on a number of issues, which were not evident to any of us at the time. War is indeed not a time for impartial judgments, and when Lanz left there was an outburst of relief and rejoicing. The news was shouted from village to village and reached us almost as quickly as a wireless signal. The bells were rung and Costakis led the whole village into church for a service of thanksgiving to praise the Lord for our survival. I was reminded of the church in Plaisia where I had been on the previous Christmas Eve, four days after my arrival. By now I could follow the service, join in the responses, bless the day that I had been born, and offer every particle of gratitude within me for the God-given opportunity to have followed the long journey that had started in Cairo and was ending in Tseritsana.

That evening we all packed up and prepared ourselves to depart the following morning as soon as the sun was up. Apart from Maniakis and Georgia, Mulholland, Katsikakis and Kalousis, our party included Leon Tsombos and Loukia Polimenou, Vassilis Derekas and Constantinos Economou – the Cherub team which had worked with such ingenuity and perseverance without any let-up during the last nine months. I was also quietly approached by Costakis, who made a special request, 'as I had been one of their family' and had 'eaten bread and salt with them', that I should take their young son, Achilleas, with me. All his life he had dreamed of his first sight of Ioannina.

Five

That mid-October day was as warm as early summer. During the seven-hour march with our mule train towards Ioannina, we made stops in several of the villages we passed on our way. At each there was a minor celebration followed by lighting a candle in the church. The whole day seemed like an extended picnic. In the early evening we saw the minarets and stately Turkish houses of Ioannina as we reached the outskirts of town. When we turned into the first street I heard music that made me doubt the evidence of my ears. I could not believe it was Bach. But then we passed a house where a prewar gramophone was playing an old cracked record of 'Jesu, Joy of Man's Desiring': a symbolic remnant, perhaps, of the German occupation. I was so deeply moved that I felt like falling on my knees.

Ours was one of the first parties to reach Ioannina, which meant we were allotted a big house by the EDES Committee. It seemed like a palace after Tseritsana, and we felt we were living the life of kings when we joined the other groups that had come down from Lakka Souli at a dinner in our honour that evening. In the next few days we prepared for Zervas's triumphal entry, which was well staged. He rode in with Pyromaglou, Barnes and his senior commanders to cheering crowds and took the salute on horseback in the main square as the culmination of a military parade which passed off without a hitch. There followed days of euphoria, wild rejoicing and a continuous succession of parties, while Zervas was acclaimed all over Epirus and visited Corfu.

It looked as if it was the end of the affair – at least for the time being – and in any case it seemed to be the end of my mission. I was therefore all the more astonished to receive an urgent signal from the Greek office on 23 October that 'now was the crucial test' of all my efforts, that this was no time to relax, and, finally, that it was not understood why I had not come forward with plans for myself, Maniakis and Kalousis to make our way to Albania and follow the progress of Lanz's retreat. Almost as an afterthought, it was added that unless I had 'overriding reasons' for not doing so, it was preferable to use even my compromised code than to withhold information.

I read this instruction with astonishment. It never occurred to me even to propose to either Maniakis or Kalousis that we should start an Albanian adventure. If I had done so, they would have thought my head needed examination, since no regular Greek officer would have contemplated accepting such an order when his country was on the eve of total liberation. As I knew that the Greek office would very shortly be arriving in Athens, and as I also did not want to compound the error of discussing operational matters in a compromised code, I signalled back that I was sending my reply by safe hand to GHQ in Athens.

In my answer I let off steam and asked first why this moment had been chosen to change their own instructions, dated 1 July, not to extend my organization into southern Albania, when I had had the opportunity to do so. Second, I inquired whether any British mission in Albania could guarantee our safe entry and security. Third, I reminded them that I would need at least a hundred sovereigns before embarking on this enterprise. I did not have these funds and was not prepared to ask Barnes to advance me a loan. There had been more than enough embarrassment of this sort in the past when he had been obliged to bail me out. Finally, I concluded that the whole project seemed completely unworkable and should never have been signalled to me in a compromised code. This and much else I wished to discuss personally with the Greek office as soon as it was set up in Athens.

In the meantime Papandreou's government and General Scobie, with the first British contingent consisting of the 23rd Armoured Brigade and attachments, had reached Athens on 18 October, some five days after the last German soldier had left the capital. This opportunity for EAM/ELAS to seize power in the interim was not taken for a mixture of reasons: the presence of Communists in Papandreou's government of National Unity; divided opinion in the KKE leadership; uncertainty about the size of the oncoming British forces; and a reluctance to engage in armed confrontation with the police and Security Battalions. On their arrival, Papandreou and Scobie drove straight to the Acropolis to hoist the Greek flag and then attended a thanksgiving service in Athens Cathedral. Papandreou's first speech from a hotel balcony was well received by a crowd with placards showing EAM/ELAS slogans, as well as 'Long Live the Allies'. But the greatest applause came when he spoke the sentence, 'We believe in the people's sovereignty [laokratia]'. For the next few days more attention was understandably paid to victory celebrations, such as we were ourselves enjoying in Ioannina, than to the most urgent problems of demobilizing EAM/ELAS and EDES, creating a new currency and restarting the national economy virtually from scratch.

On 7 November I received orders to report to the Greek office in person. It took me four days to reach Athens in a journey involving EDES transport from Ioannina to Preveza, whence the Navy kindly took me to the port of Piraeus. On the way I was preparing a series of set speeches for what I anticipated would be an angry first encounter with the head of the Greek office. It was therefore something of an anticlimax to find that he was not prepared to press his earlier arguments and I was told that the instruction to launch out into Albania had originated in GHQ. I was asked to forget the whole incident as a trivial misunderstanding, and in return it was agreed that my mission should be wound up without delay and that all those who had so faithfully collaborated with us would receive generous treatment. On this score I had no problems, as every one of my proposals was accepted without argument.

The head of the Greek office appeared, however, to be in difficulties when we turned to more fundamental questions. First, I asked about my predecessor, whom Spike Moran had shot. Had any further information come their way justifying the action taken by SOE? Or was it still thought that the charges against Costa Lawrence had been trumped up? But he was not to be drawn and refused then or later to discuss the matter. Next I asked for an evaulation of the incident that had so plainly indicated that my codes had been compromised. How had the experts in this field reacted? What were SOE's observations? In answer to these questions I was told that it appeared that the key phrase in my letter transposition code had been overworked with the heavy traffic I had been sending and ought to have been changed much sooner. It was admitted that this had been a mistake; but I was given no clear answer to my question whether there had been an exchange of information on this subject with SOE. I had left to the last the most important matter of all, so far as I was concerned. I introduced it by retailing my conversation with David Wallace and citing his evidence that my political reports had not been seen by him either in the Foreign Office or the British Embassy in Cairo. In that event, I asked, what had happened to them? To whom had they been distributed? If to no one, why had they been buried? In any case, why had I been given no indication of their value? If it was considered that I had been reporting rubbish, why had I not been reprimanded?

The head of the Greek office cut short my questions by informing me that in the first place all this was none of my business. His orders had been to send my political reports only to GHQ. The absence of comment was therefore explained by the fact that the military could claim no special competence in the political field; but when this statement provoked me into asking again why my reports had been withheld from the British Embassy, which might be presumed to be the competent authority for political evaluation, I was given no answer. (On my first visit to the head office of SIS in London in January 1945, the head of the Political Section informed me that not one of my political reports had reached him.) When I said that the immediate future mattered more than raking over the past and that consequently I wished to be put in touch with the Embassy and with Scobie, I was told that this would be arranged on my next visit.

This visit, however, afforded me my first sight of Athens since I had raced through the city in a convoy retreating from the Germans in April 1941. It was also an opportunity to link up with some old friends and to make new ones through a handful of introductions to Athenians that had been given me by Costas Achillopoulos, with who I had kept in close touch since his arrival in Tseritsana in August. In this way every moment of five full days was spent in a happy return to a normal life under my own name. I found it a blessed relief to drop the play-acting associated with my role as Captain Jim and to know that in so short a while all this would be behind me. Athens at that time was a most welcoming city. The last German troops had left mainland Greece on 5 November and this in itself provided the best of reasons for riotous celebration. A new life with new people was beginning. But the gaiety was mixed with apprehension, because virtually no one I met believed in the possibility of a peaceful evolution of events. (Almost the only exception was the *Times* correspondent, Geoffrey Hoare, whose reporting consistently favoured EAM/ELAS.) The issue was not if, but when, the clash would occur. My newly acquired Athenian friends, most of whom claimed to have been associated in some form with the Resistance during the German occupation, had widely different political affiliations. They were split between royalists and republicans and between right-wing Populists and left-wing Liberals. But they all shared three views: that EAM/ELAS would make a bid for power; that British policy was the root cause of what had happened in mountain Greece since the start of the resistance in 1942 (this was a facile interpretation but not one with which it was easy to argue at that juncture); and that Scobie would soon have a battle on his hands in which British troops would be involved.

On 16 November I flew back to Ioannina in a seaplane which landed us on the lake. During the flight we ran into a violent storm with such heavy clouds that the pilot was forced to fly very low and follow the road between the hills from Arta to Ioannina. This caused us a number of anxious moments, as the seaplane was not constructed to fly a course of sudden twists and turns. As I had learned the geography of this area pretty well, I was able to offer the pilot some minimal assistance, but there was more than one occasion before we saw the lake at Ioannina when we were flying blind and knew there was every likelihood that we would crash into the hillside. For the second time – the first time being the sea crossing from Alexandria to Piraeus in March 1941 – I was reminded that there could have been few more unsatisfying ways of meeting death in time of war. But whether by chance or the pilot's skill we were spared.

It was a happy experience to be back in Ioannina and to dole out to our agents and their associates gold sovereigns and certificates signed by Field Marshal Alexander for 'valuable contributions to the Allied cause'. Of course, the sovereigns were more than acceptable as the only currency worth owning, but the certificates were the equivalent of medals and were highly prized. I chose carefully those who had earned them and only selected individuals who had risked their necks at some stage. Others, who had provided some kind of auxiliary service, came forward with protests that they had been excluded. But I had no serious incidents. The Greek agent, well known to have worked for the Sicherheitsdienst, who had given the Cherub group the vital warning to escape, had been legitimately arrested by EDES as a German collaborator. I had, however, no difficulty in securing his immediate release when I explained to Zervas how well he had been serving us for the past six months. As my mission was closing down, Kalousis and Katsikakis duly reported back to Greek Army headquarters in Athens and Maniakis rejoined EDES in Ioannina. This was a most fortunate link in view of what happened later. When the fighting broke out in Athens in December 1944, ELAS attacked all EDES-held territory, and quickly forced Zervas to retreat to Corfu. But Maniakis was able to insure that the Cherub team and other close collaborators of Kalousis were safely evacuated to Corfu with the EDES units. When all my obligations had been fulfilled, I had my last meeting with Barnes to inform him that my mission was finished and that I was on my way to Athens. Warm handshakes and mutual expressions of gratitude brought our close collaboration throughout 1944 to a happy end.

With Zervas, I had a long final conversation on 19 November. I began by thanking him for my protection in EDES territory and the constant help his organization had provided. But before I had completed these courtesies, he cut me short and asked, knowing that I had recently been in Athens, whether Scobie and the British Embassy had a satisfactory political understanding of the present precarious situation. He said he could not foretell when EAM/ELAS would make their bid for power. The only certainty was that it would happen sometime soon. While he said that he approved Papandreou's order for the demobilization of all guerrilla forces, he made the obvious point that it would serve neither Greek nor Allied interests if EDES was to be disbanded while EAM/ELAS remained intact. He repeated that he would be prepared to meet Scobie to discuss demobilization – the meeting was in fact arranged in the following week – but he wanted to know in what frame of mind he would find him. I had to reply, somewhat tamely, that I would not be seeing Scobie until my next visit and added, trying to hide a blush, that I was sure the British authorities had a clear understanding of the situation. The conversation then turned to a string of reminiscences and to our first meeting almost a year earlier at his headquarters in Derviziana. For the first and only time he made mention of Lawrence and thanked me for what I had done to make amends for my predecessor. As I got up to go, he made a final plea that I should speak firmly as soon as I returned to Athens and said that we should keep in touch, as he would shortly be there himself.

I also took leave of Pyromaglou and found him in a mood to give me his version of what he called the 'lost opportunities of the British' for organizing a united resistance. I had heard this criticism from him often before and its repetition did not surprise me. Nor was it surprising to hear him hark back to the fundamental error of British policy, which stemmed, in his view, from HMG's unconditional support of the King. This, too, had been a constant theme since our first meeting. But now he thought that it was too late to retrieve the errors of the past and he, like Zervas, considered that the only issue of the moment was when ELAS would choose to fight it out. As he also knew that I had recently come back from Athens, he was anxious to learn what kind of a reputation, both military and political, EDES had established with Scobie and the British Embassy. Once again I had to find excuses for the fact that I had not been in Athens for political consultations. When at the end I asked him what political future he foresaw for Zervas, he humped his broad shoulders and raised his arms in a gesture that demonstrated the height of his uncertainty. This was the last I saw of him in his role as Zervas's political adviser.

I returned from Ioannina via Arta and Preveza in order to pay off our agents in the towns and distribute the Alexander certificates. From there the Navy gave me a lift to Patras and I reached Athens again on 24 November. The Greek office quickly put me in touch with Harold Caccia, who had been appointed by Harold Macmillan to act as Scobie's political adviser. I reported to him my last conversations with Zervas and Pyromaglou and took the opportunity to give a full account of how I had watched the political situation develop since my arrival in Greece nearly a year before. He listened attentively and then fired back a list of legitimate questions. I was handicapped in my answers because I was unable to quote from personal experience of EAM/ELAS. Caccia said that his problem was the plethora of reports that were reaching him, most but not all of which confirmed my assessment that EAM/ELAS was prepared to take the final risk. It was, however, clearly in Zervas's interest to press the case that his enemy was on the point of trying to seize power. To what extent was this special pleading? He told me that Scobie was virtually convinced that British forces would very soon be involved and that Papandreou's scepticism about persuading the Communist and EAM ministers in his government to sign the demobilization decree verged on disbelief. This, he said, was also the British Ambassador's view. I said that even if the Ministers signed the demobilization decree, their signatures could and would be denounced by EAM/ELAS in a matter of hours. Caccia agreed this was likely. He asked if I believed it had been a mistake to allow the Mountain (Rimini) Brigade, formed in the aftermath of the mutiny in Egypt during April, and the Sacred Brigade, both of which had fought so well in Italy, to return to Athens earlier that month. It had been put to him, he said, that their presence, more than anything else, had destroyed what remained of EAM/ ELAS belief in British good faith. I said I thought EAM was using the presence of these formations as a convenient excuse not to demobilize ELAS.

On 28 November I saw Zervas in Athens for the last time while I was in uniform. It was a brief meeting and there seemed little to be said. At this juncture he was understandably on edge and deeply apprehensive about ELAS's intentions. His normal ebullience was suppressed. Indeed, he wondered whether the whole of his struggle had been in vain. He gave me, as he had given to others, a photograph of himself, mounted on his charger with Barnes at his side, taking the salute at the EDES victory parade in Ioannina the previous month and wrote on it in Greek: 'To my collaborator Captain Jim Russell in memory of our life in the mountains.' This was the last time I was addressed by my pseudonym.

Between 26 and 27 November Scobie made three abortive attempts to disarm the guerrilla organizations. On 29 November Zevgos and Porphyrogenis, two of the Communist Ministers in Papandreou's government, refused to sign the demobilization order and on 1 December *Rizospastis*, the Communist newspaper, printed an article by Zevgos which was a call to arms and an order to stop further negotiations with Papandreou. On the same day the Town Committee of the Communist Organization of Athens issued a proclamation stating:

A great and immediate danger threatens our country. The opposition is organizing a coup d'état to restore the King to power and to reinstate a Monarcho-Fascist dictatorship. ELAS stands as an invincible obstacle to the carrying out of this new crime at the people's expense. This is why they are trying to dissolve ELAS. People of Athens, stand by with your arms.

Scobie immediately issued an order of the day calling on all officers and men of the Greek Resistance to carry out the instructions of the Greek government in an orderly and soldier-like manner, after which they would be at liberty to return with honour to their homes. This order was printed on a leaflet and dropped from the air all over Greece. It was also broadcast on Athens radio. In this proclamation Scobie stressed that he would stand firmly behind the present constitutional government until such time as the Greek state could be established with legal armed force behind it and elections could be held. Otherwise the currency would not remain stable and the people would not be fed. He would protect the government against any attempt at a coup d'état or any act of violence. On 2 December Churchill issued the following statement from Downing Street: 'The Prime Minister wishes it to be known that General Scobie's message of 1st December to the Greek people, stressing the need for unity and emphasizing our full support of the present Greek Government was made with the knowledge and entire approval of H.M. Government.'

The Civil Guard, which was EAM's police force, had also refused on 1 December to hand over their weapons to the newly formed National Guard on the grounds that no agreement had been reached on demobilization. This led Papandreou to draft a decree for signature by all the Ministers in his government ordering the Civil Guard to hand in their arms. On this issue the government split. It surprised neither Papandreou nor Leeper that the draft decree was not signed by the six EAM Ministers in the government; by 2 December Svolos, Tsirimokos, Angelopoulos, Askoutsis, Zevgos and Porphyrogenis had all resigned. After that there could be no doubt that civil war was imminent.

On 2 December the Central Committee of EAM took the decision to organize a major demonstration in Constitution Square in Athens for the following day and to proclaim a general strike on 4 December. It was also decided to reconstitute the Central Committee of ELAS and to send an appeal to the British, Russian and American governments. After some hesitation Papandreou finally decided to ban the demonstration, but EAM accepted the challenge and went ahead with their preparations. In the meanwhile ELAS started infiltrating Athens and Piraeus.

As I was on duty in the Greek office on 3 December I did not witness any of the events of that historic Sunday morning, which finally triggered the start of the Second Round of the Greek Civil War.[20] The day began with headlines in *Rizospastis* calling on the people to join EAM's demonstration in Constitution Square with the slogans 'Down with the Government of Civil War' and 'Forward to a Government of Real National Unity'. Once more Zevgos wrote a fierce leading article ending: 'Now the time has come for the Greek people to speak for the powder-blackened fighters of ELAS who are being asked to give up their honoured and battle-won weapons.' It was only after lunch time that day that I heard of the grenades being thrown and the shooting near Papandreou's house during the morning. Meantime, a massive, disciplined group of demonstrators had begun to assemble in Constitution Square, carrying the flags of Greece, Britain, Russia and the United States, singing Resistance songs and shouting EAM slogans. An inevitable clash with the police led to casualties on both sides. Later there was controversy as to who fired first and consequently as to which side had a legitimate claim to martyrdom. Subsequent research has not led to definite responsi-

[20] See the detailed analysis of the demonstration in Constitution Square by Lars Baerentzen in *Scandinavian Studies in Modern Greek*, no.2 (1978).

bility being pinned on either side; but at the time, and in retrospect, this seemed an almost academic issue. If the revolution had not got under way with this incident, another would have been chosen. Since, however, the first shots from the police had brought the advancing column to a halt, their failure to cease firing at that point was a political mistake.

Fortunately, Scobie's troops were not involved in the incident. British tanks and lorries did not appear on the scene until later that morning and were greeted with applause. At the same time Dimitrios Partsalides, the Secretary General of EAM, speaking from the Communist party (KKE) building opposite the Grande Bretagne Hotel in Constitution Square, denounced Papandreou as an outlaw and called on the people to fight for liberty without counting their sacrifices.

The crowd then broke up into smaller groups and marched off in different directions shouting 'Long live Democracy, long live Churchill, down with Papandreou' and – as a constant refrain from one group outside the American Embassy – 'Long live Roosevelt'. This could have provided some satisfaction to Ambassador Lincoln MacVeagh, whose neutrality was common knowledge and was advertised with advantage by a number of Americans, including some of their foreign correspondents. A most notable exception, however, was the Ambassador's cousin, Shan Sedgwick, whose comprehensive reporting to the *New York Times* before, during and after these events, had shown no grain of sympathy for EAM and a clear understanding of British policy.

In his broadcast on the night of 3 December, Papandreou put the blame for what had happened on the Communists. The next day there were numerous attacks on police stations in Athens, and on 5 December Scobie ordered full offensive action, backed by Churchill's order to him – which soon became well known – 'to act as if you were in a conquered city where a local rebellion is in progress'.[21] Sporadic fighting escalated over the next two days as ELAS attacked police stations and government buildings throughout Athens.

In London, there was a heated debate in the House of Commons, ending on 9 December, with Nye Bevan and Seymour

[21] Winston Churchill, *The Second World War*, vol. 6 (Cassells, 1954), p.252.

Cocks leading the attack on Churchill's policy. 'On the sacred soil of Athens,' said Cocks, 'in the shadow of the Acropolis British soldiers and Greek patriots lie dead, side by side, each with an Allied bullet in his heart, and I ask the Government to put an end immediately to this fratricidal strife. I would like to point out that EAM is not a Communist Party. It is supported by ninety per cent of the population of Greece, according to *The Times*. The military wing, known as ELAS, has fought hard and well against the Germans.' His version of the shooting in Constitution Square was based on the reports of Geoffrey Hoare, the *Times* correspondent, who had said that the presence of British units had served to associate Britain with what was everywhere condemned as fascist action. I was soon to see the follow-up to this debate when I went back to London.

Costas Achillopoulos had taken me to meet some friends in the evening of 4 December. Our discussions had lasted late into the night, when we heard a brisk exchange of fire near the Stadium. Nobody asked what it meant. Shooting on that scale showed that the fight would have to be carried to a finish. As it would have been lunacy to go out on the street, everyone stayed for the night and slept on the floor. It was a reminder of similar, but happier, recent occasions in the mountains when we were celebrating on the eve of the German withdrawal. In the morning I made my way back to the Greek office and was told to report to Scobie's headquarters without delay. From there I was posted as a liaison officer with the Greek government, which was settled in the Grande Bretagne Hotel on Constitution Square in the centre of Athens. During the next week we had a severe problem in trying to hold even the central perimeter of Athens. As there had been no operational plan prepared for an ELAS attack, the RAF headquarters had been pitched in Kifissia, outside Athens (an inexplicable blunder), which allowed it to be captured on 15 December.

These were anxious and exciting days. I shuttled to and from the Grande Bretagne with messages to Papandreou from Scobie urging him to keep his spirits up. My job was, in fact, to be little more than a postman, as I was under strict orders not to engage in any form of political discussion. But in the afternoon of 10 December, when the battle was at its height and it was plain that it would take time and reinforcements before ELAS could be pushed back, Papandreou summoned me and sat me down for a chat. He was worried and depressed and even went so far as to wonder whether ELAS was on the point of outright victory. I naturally replied that this was unthinkable, and tried to comfort him by saying that reinforcements of Scobie's command were on their way. Even from my short acquaintance with Papandreou, I knew that histrionic gestures came naturally to him, but this time I could see that he was not putting on an act when he strode towards the window and gazed out over Constitution Square, murmuring, 'When will they come? When will they come? Tell Scobie I must know the date, and if it's not soon, it will be too late. Go and speak to him now and don't return without an answer.' Usually I carried written communications like a normal postman, but on this occasion I had to report that his morale was faltering. I came back, of course, with no satisfactory news for Papandreou, but while I was waiting to see Scobie I was handed a message from the Greek office asking me to contact them for an urgent assignment.

On 8 December Scobie had received a telegram from ELAS, signed by Saraphis, protesting against the intervention of British troops but laying the principal blame on Papandreou for starting the Civil War. On 9 December, Scobie replied to Saraphis repudiating all the charges laid against himself and Papandreou. On 10 December, when the Greek office sent for me, it was to announce that EAM had telephoned to one of our contacts, who had been part of a large intelligence group in Athens throughout the German occupation, saying that they would be prepared to send a member of the Central Committee – the name was not specified – for a meeting with Scobie, if a British officer in uniform was sent as escort. I was asked if I would accept the job. The Greek intermediary turned out to be Stamatis Merkouris, a prominent prewar Liberal deputy, the son of a well-known Mayor of Athens and the father of Melina, the actress and Minister of Culture in the 1981 government of Andreas Papandreou, himself the son of the Prime Minister of that time. When I called the number that had been left at the end of the message from EAM (the telephone system worked perfectly throughout the Battle of Athens) an unidentified voice proposed, and I agreed, subject to Scobie's concurrence, that a meeting should take place in the underground in Omonia Square at 10.30 on 12 December. As we both knew, this was no man's land, with British troops exchanging fire with ELAS from opposite sides of the square. EAM had proposed a temporary cease-fire beginning at 10.15 and lasting until 12.30. It was a polite conversation without invective of any sort on either side. After clearance by GHQ, I telephoned again to EAM to confirm the timing of the cease-fire. It was a strange experience, in the middle of a battle, to ring up the enemy.

On 12 December at ten o'clock a jeep with a large white flag drove Stamatis Merkouris and myself to a forward sandbagged position held by British parachutists on the edge of Omonia Square. The officer in charge had received his orders and was expecting us. The shooting was brisk, as we had arrived a good ten minutes before the agreed time of the cease-fire. Punctually at 10.15, he issued his order and there was an instant response from the other side of the square. I thought it wise to allow a little extra time, in case of accidents, and then walked across the square and into the underground station, accompanied by Merkouris. There we met three unarmed members of ELAS with whom we exchanged formal greetings. Two of them escorted me alone up the exit from the underground on the far side of the square, and then led me in a short walk to a ground floor flat, which was heavily guarded. No word was exchanged on either side.

There I found a group of people sitting round a table and arguing hard as we entered. I saluted the gathering and asked if their representative was ready to accompany me back to meet Scobie. This rather stiff introduction produced a warm invitation to sit down and join them for coffee. The first to speak and to announce his name was Porphyrogenis, one of the Communist Ministers who had refused to sign the demobilization order. He made no tirade against Scobie and merely mourned the fact that British troops were fighting Greeks. A volley of questions from him and others was then rattled off. Why was Scobie tied to Papandreou? Did we not see that Papandreou was the cause of all the trouble? Was it Churchill or Scobie who still insisted on supporting Papandreou? What were Scobie's objectives? How would it all end? I was expecting a questionnaire of this nature and had to disappoint them with the reply that I was under strict orders not to engage in a political discussion. Seeing that there was nothing to be learned from someone so uninformative, Porphyrogenis ended this short meeting and we made our way back to Omonia Square, where fortunately the cease-fire was still being observed on both sides.

His meeting with Scobie and Harold Caccia led to nothing and did not last long. Porphyrogenis reproduced all EAM's charges against what could arguably have been claimed to be Papandreou's bad faith when he appeared to shift his ground on the establishment of a new military formation, which would have been remarkably favourable to EAM/ELAS.[22] Porphyrogenis's only positive statement was to assert that he would be authorized, in the name of KKE/EAM/ELAS, to call off the fight if the aged prewar Liberal leader Sophoulis replaced Papandreou. But Scobie had no authority even to initiate negotiations for a political settlement and least of all to tamper with the composition of the Greek government. He twice demanded the withdrawal of ELAS from Attica and the surrender of their units in Athens and Piraeus. Porphyrogenis said he had not come to GHQ in order to surrender, and tried to turn the conversation back to Papandreou. It was soon plain that no purpose was being served by continuing the discussion.

When it broke up, I took Porphyrogenis back to Omonia Square and handed him over to his friends, who were waiting for him in the underground. As he approached them, they could not restrain themselves from shouting the obvious questions. How did it go? Any results? But he remained tight-lipped. I shook his hand, saluted and made my way back across the square. When I reached the advance post manned by British parachutists, the officer in charge asked me if any agreement had been reached, and if not, when the battle could be expected to begin again. His orders were not to shoot first. I said that he would not have to wait long. I heard the first exchange of shots in the jeep as we were driving back to Scobie's headquarters.

The morning's break had been a brief interlude. By lunch time the fighting had started again with full force on both sides. I had

[22] See G. M. Alexander, *The Prelude to the Truman Doctrine: British Policy in Greece, 1944-1947* (Clarendon Press, 1982), pp. 74-6.

not thought that there was one chance in a million of EAM/ ELAS calling off the battle, which at that moment they were plainly winning. Nor, of course, was there the slightest chance that Scobie would give in, although we were only holding a perimeter in the heart of Athens and very little more. An armoured convoy was needed on the main road down to the aerodrome by the sea and the port of Piraeus. Both rations and ammunition were low. No one contemplated a catastrophe, but we knew we were in a precarious state of siege.

This was plain to Field Marshal Alexander and Harold Macmillan when they flew in from Caserta on 11 December and were shocked by what they found. Alexander's immediate impulse was to sack Scobie on the spot; he was only prevented from doing so by an astute intervention of Rex Leeper, the British Ambassador, who said rightly that Scobie's public dismissal would be a victory in itself for ELAS. So it was agreed that he should be left formally in overall control, but in fact the command of the ground operations was handed to Major General Hawkesworth, whom Alexander summoned from Italy. 'Ginger' Hawkesworth arrived on 15 December, and it was he who defeated ELAS and won the Battle of Athens; but it was Scobie who got the lion's share of the credit from most Greeks as their liberator (from 'the Second Occupation') both then and thereafter.

The excitement of those days left me neither the time nor the inclination to keep anything more than bare jottings in my personal diary. In the evenings after the to and fro between the Greek government offices in the Grande Bretagne Hotel and GHQ, I spent my time in getting to know many Athenians whose political affiliations were often radically different, such as the republican Liberal, Stamatis Merkouris, and the royalist Populists, Spiros Theotokis and his father Ioannis. We would gather in one flat and drift to another in meetings which had no beginning and no end, and where anxiety was spiced with gaiety. Sporadic sniper fire was continuous even in the non-ELAS-controlled parts of Athens. I had seen in the mountains that Greeks were the least morose people imaginable, notably in times of adversity. At the height of the Battle of Athens, I never saw a trace of gloom. There was well-founded apprehension and uncertainty, but the predominant feeling was one of confidence. Having survived the German occupation, it was unthinkable to Athenians that they could not live through the temporary nightmare of EAM/ELAS. Political argument continued until late into the night; it was always serious and vigorous, but had a charm of its own by being punctuated with moments of hilarity and explosions of laughter.

For me, this was the end of the first part of my life in Greece. A telegram had come through from London ordering me to report for consultations and I saw the happy prospect of my first Christmas at home for four years. I longed to be in England, but I knew that all I needed was a temporary break and I would soon want to be back. I flew out on 20 December 1944, which was almost exactly a year since I had dropped by parachute into Epirus. After a brief stay in Caserta I reached home on Christmas morning, to hear on the radio that Churchill and Eden had just arrived in Athens. I missed all that, but such was my relief to be in London again that for a short while, a very short while, I was happy to be away from it all.

Six

In London, I found virtually all my friends bewildered and disturbed by the Greek situation from which I had just emerged. Most of them were passionately opposed to Churchill's policy, believing that there could have been no justification on earth for British troops to be ordered to shoot against 'the same Greeks who a few months ago were fighting the Germans'. In any event, the weird vocabulary of names, initials and organizations could not be memorized and correctly categorized even by those with a professional interest in trying to follow what was happening. The message in leading articles in *The Times*, masterminded by E. H. Carr, later the historian of Soviet Russia, and supported by its correspondent in Athens, was hard to distinguish from that of the editorials in the *New Statesman*. The feeling was widespread that crimes compounded with blunders were being committed in Athens.

Robin Barrington-Ward, the editor of *The Times*, happened to be a friend of my father. Early in January 1945 the three of us lunched together at the Garrick and in no time we had pitched into a humourless argument. Barrington-Ward opened with the simple thesis that Churchill had gone off his head – not for the first time in his political life – by ordering British troops to intervene in Athens. This showed that the war had taught him nothing. It was obvious that he was trying to impose a politically and morally untenable regime, against the expressed wish of the Greek people, which could not anyhow be expected to survive more than a few weeks in the postwar world. Crazier still was Churchill's choice of the Greek issue to foul up his relations with Roosevelt and Stalin, both of whom had criticized British action in Athens. He had done so merely to satisfy a personal whim. The policy we were following in Greece showed Churchill's profound misjudgment of British interests, which would become even more apparent when the war was over.

Memorial at Arta to the fallen, 1941–45

Typical terrain in Lakka Souli

The author with (seated, right) Costakis, owner of the house,
and (left) Spiro, the cook. Behind stand Costakis's wife and daughter,
Niko, the mule driver, and Aristides, the runner

The author with Mario Maniakis

Spike Moran

C. M. Woodhouse

Zervas taking the salute at the victory parade in Ioannina, October 1944. The inscription reads, in translation: 'To my collaborator Captain Jim Russell, in memory of our life in the mountains. Athens 28.11.44'

Tom Barnes

Zervas, Tom Barnes and Pyromaglou (right)
riding into Ioannina, October 1944

Maria, crossing Constitution Square the day before the shooting started

TUESDAY, DECEMBER 5, 1944
FINAL NIGHT EXTRA

In the family tradition
BIRD'S CUSTARD

Evening Standard

For Inner Warmth
WILLIAM YOUNGERS Scotch Ale

37,513   DIM-OUT: 5.22 pm to 8.20 am   MOON: Rises 10.38 pm; Sets 1.35 pm   ONE PENNY

Churchill: Greeks Must Decide for Themselves, But—

BRITISH ARMY WILL KEEP
ORDER IN ATHENS

Our Troops Are Acting To Prevent Bloodshed

Until the Greek people are in a position of deciding on the form of their government "we shall not hesitate to use the considerable British Army now in Greece, and being reinforced, to see that law and order are being maintained."

MR. CHURCHILL MADE THIS DECLARATION IN PARLIAMENT TO-DAY IN A STATEMENT ON THE OCCURRENCES IN ATHENS.

HE ADDED:

" Whether the Greek people form themselves into a monarchy or republic is for their decision ; whether they form a Government of the right or left is for their decision."

NEW GREEK CABINET IS BEING FORMED

At the outset of his statement Mr. Churchill said:
" So far as has been ascertained, the facts are as follows:
" The Greek organisation E.A.M. had announced their intention of holding a demonstration on December 3.
" The Greek Government at first authorised this, but withdrew their permission when E.A.M. called for a general strike to begin on December 2. The strike, in fact, came into force early on December 3.
" Later in the morning the E.A.M. demonstration formed up, and moved to the principal square of Athens, in spite of the Government's ban.
" On the evidence so far available I am not prepared to say who started the firing which then

London Will

CHRISTMAS TRAVEL
No Extra Trains

Lord Leathers, Minister of War Transport, in view of Service needs, has decided that additional long-distance passenger trains at Christmas cannot be provided.
Where trains are withdrawn owing to the holidays, the equivalent may be made up by the provision of a limited number of release trains on other routes.

Supplies for Saar Blasted

BOMBERS IN GREAT STRENGTH, FOLLOWING A 36-HOUR NON-STOP ATTACK ON GERMANY, FLEW OUT OVER THE EAST COAST BEFORE IT WAS LIGHT TO-DAY. SHORTLY AFTER, ALL THE GERMAN MEDIUM-WAVE STATIONS WERE OFF THE AIR.

More than 3500 tons of bombs were dropped by R.A.F. Bomber Command in last night's attack on Heilbronn and Karlsruhe—two railway centres which must have been packed with supplies and reserves being rushed up to the Saar.

Karlsruhe is the nearest large town to the south-western front, where the United States 7th Army is pounding at the Nazi defences.

"Solid Fire"

Both attacks begin simultaneously. There was some cloud along the route and over the target, but most of the aiming points were identified and accurately marked by flares. Bombing was concentrated, and large fires were seen to be during a firm hold.
At Heilbronn, fighters were up in great numbers and there were several combats.
Besides these two heavy attacks, the transport centre of Hagen, some 15 miles south of Dortmund, was also bombed.
Returning crews reported that

Headlines in the London *Evening Standard*, 5 December 1944

Return to Tseritsana, 1973

It was some time before I was allowed to get a word in edgeways as a sequel to this monologue. When I was given the opportunity to speak, I asked Barrington-Ward to pinpoint the political party or parties that were valid representatives of the Greek people, for whom he had expressed such concern and admiration. He replied that this was rather like asking a Yugoslav if he had heard of Tito. As he had understood from my father that I had spent the whole of 1944 in Greece, it mystified him that I had not grasped the significance of EAM/ELAS. Without any success, I tried to explain the situation in somewhat different terms, and suggested to him the unwisdom of accepting the credentials of self-styled representatives of the people. Any election conducted with the minimum safeguards for a free vote would, I forecast, produce results that would astound him. But Barrington-Ward was not impressed. After he had left us at the end of an utterly sterile debate, I was reminded that he had turned aside my father's tentative proposal to him early in 1938 that I might join *The Times* when I came down from Oxford. Later in the year he had given as his reason the part I had played in the Oxford by-election in October 1938 (just after Munich) when, as President of the Carlton Club that term, I had actively campaigned for the Master of Balliol against Quintin Hogg, the Conservative candidate who supported unconditionally Chamberlain's foreign policy. In view of the editorial policy of *The Times* in 1938, it was only to be expected that Barrington-Ward considered my stance to be unpardonable. My father remembered, however, his remark when I had signed a letter with others (including Ted Heath) opposing Quintin Hogg that was published in the *News Chronicle*: 'The Times is no place for hotheads of any age.' There was a certain irony in this statement when placed against what he had just been saying.

On 18 January 1945 Alan Lennox-Boyd took me down to the House of Commons to hear Churchill open the two-day debate on Greece and I dined that night with Harold Nicolson and Desmond Shawe-Taylor, who had been on the staff of the *New Statesman* before the war. They both wanted to hear about my experience in Greece and, in contradistinction to my meeting with Barrington-Ward, I was made to do all the talking to an understanding audience. At the end they jointly suggested that I should have a discussion with Kingsley Martin, the editor of the *New Statesman*, and proposed that he should be approached through Raymond Mortimer, who was then the literary editor and a close friend of them both. Shortly afterwards Kingsley Martin telephoned to suggest that I should have a frank exchange of views with him and some of his colleagues. I agreed on condition that he would not quote me by name, as I was still in uniform. This undertaking was given and upheld.

We met for lunch in Soho. Kingsley Martin had with him, among other colleagues from the *New Statesman*, Dorothy Woodman, Aylmer Vallance and Leonard Woolf. Before the soup was served, questions had been put that showed the way in which the discussion would develop. I was asked what it had felt like to be a British officer in EDES territory where there had been German officers in uniform attached to Zervas's headquarters. Since Zervas was as much of a Quisling as Mihailovic, what justification could I offer for the active participation of British officers in traitorous acts of collaboration with the enemy? What were the relations between British and German officers in Epirus? Had it not seemed strange to both sides that Zervas provided the common ground on which we met?

To this opening salvo I replied that I had indeed met a number of German officers and other ranks during my time in Epirus. Our relationship had been governed by the fact that they were all either prisoners or deserters, and my interest in talking to them was exclusively confined to extracting the best information I could gather on the German order of battle for the benefit of GHQ in Cairo. I thought that Hitler might have found this to be a somewhat odd form of collaboration.

My short answer produced a gale of laughter. Everything I had said seemed to them pure fiction. Was this what I had been told to say to cover the truth? I then suggested to Kingsley Martin that he might wish to economize on the cost of my lunch, since it seemed a pointless exercise for them to listen to a continuation of what they would judge to be a fairy tale. There was an unhappy pause, while my host steered the conversation round to more recent events, and especially to the outbreak of the fighting in Athens. What was my explanation of Churchill's policy?

This gave me the chance to speak at some length and I was given the floor without much interruption. I drew on the political reports I had sent from Epirus which were fresh in my mind. My main points were to stress the mistakes that EAM had made and to suggest that if the Communist Party had played its hand with greater skill, it might well have achieved its primary objective of uniting and thereafter controlling the various resistance movements which had begun to take root in mountain Greece in 1943. At that time they had had the huge advantage that there was no substantial support for the King in any part of Greece, or even in Cairo in the Greek government in exile. Memories were still fresh of Metaxas's 'royalist' dictatorship. These were factors which could have been exploited if EAM/ELAS had not so brazenly followed Communist directives to smash any resistance movement it did not directly control. They had revealed their intentions far too soon and had thereby created the strength of their enemies. I told my listeners the sad story of EKKA and the murder of Psarros, which had escaped their notice. I explained the unimpeachable republican backgrounds of Zervas and Pyromaglou and added my estimate that EDES had no political shape and therefore no political future. All this had become progressively plain in 1944. It was EAM/ELAS which had held EDES together as a temporary entity in the last year of the German occupation and EAM/ELAS's crowning achievement, in the most literal sense, would be to have done more than any political personality or party to restore King George to his throne by launching their revolution in December. The principal beneficiary of the backlash would be the King himself, and if a plebiscite went in his favour, as I then thought likely, he ought to thank the Communists before anyone else, including Churchill.

The discussion took a new turn when Kingsley Martin said that my main argument was interesting but unpersuasive, because it contained a fatal flaw. I had been saying in effect that the Left had behaved so unwisely that they had served the purposes of their political opponents. It seemed clear to him that I must have distorted the facts, and I had shown in my twisted version of what had happened that I knew no history and had no grip of the historical process. With one exception, the others nodded their approval of the judge's summing up.

163

Throughout the lunch Leonard Woolf had been almost silent. He chose this moment to intervene and save me by saying what I could not say myself. Rounding on Kingsley Martin, he said that he had no means of knowing whether my account of the events had been true or false. Much of it had seemed strange to him and some of my statements and interpretations had been hard to believe. But under no circumstances could he accept that the Left was divinely protected from doing certain things, just because they were unwise or even foolish. This seemed to him rubbish as an argument and rubbish in his reading of history. Such a rejoinder left me with nothing to add or subtract and I stayed gratefully silent until the conversation turned to lighter matters. In fact, the lunch broke up in a more friendly atmosphere, especially when I said, to the astonishment of them all, that I intended to vote Labour in the first postwar election.

Seven

The events leading up to the demobilization crisis in Athens in November 1944 should have shaken the different forms of belief, so widely held, in ready-made British solutions to Greek problems. But once the fighting had begun in Athens in December, there could be no doubt on either side of the argument that Britain would assume sole responsibility for the military and political outcome. This was reinforced by Churchill's and Eden's dramatic descent on Athens over Christmas, which resulted in the rapid decision to appoint the Archbishop of Athens, Damaskinos, as Regent until a plebiscite could be held. The way for this, notably in persuading Churchill of the need to keep the King outside the political arena for the time being, had been skilfully prepared by Macmillan. Apart from sheltering a British officer, Frank Macaskie, during the occupation, Damaskinos had been in touch since 1943 with Tsouderos, the Prime Minister of the Greek government in exile in Cairo, over the possibility of forming an anti-Communist counterbloc to EAM/ELAS. His name had already been mooted in early 1944 as the best available candidate if a Regency were to be established before the King's return. But until they met, it was not known how Churchill would react to Damaskinos. In the event, he took to him immediately.

In the closing days of 1944 Damaskinos's appointment was reluctantly proclaimed from London by the King, who had been battered into agreement by Churchill: which was a most unusual role for him. The Regent's first act was to accept Papandreou's resignation. He was succeeded in early January 1945 by General Plastiras, the titular head of EDES, who formed a predominantly republican government. In mid January ELAS agreed to a truce.

Greece, though technically an independent country, was at this stage a form of British protectorate. Hence, from the start of 1945 Rex Leeper, the British Ambassador, had a range of powers and responsibilities more akin to those of a colonial governor than to the head of a normal diplomatic mission. In his *War Diaries* Macmillan significantly referred to the clear distinction between his Allied responsibilities in Italy and his British duties in Greece.

Damaskinos and Leeper quickly formed a working partnership, with each of them in basic agreement on political objectives but sometimes differing on their means of achievement. Leeper operated in tandem with Macmillan and all three of them saw that the first priority, after General Hawkesworth's victory in Athens, was not to lose the peace after winning the war. Leeper correctly estimated that the next round of conflict with EAM/ELAS would begin by being political. To outflank the opposition politically meant isolating the Left by building up a strong, moderate and progressive centre, whose virtues might not have an immediate appeal to an electorate shaken by war and civil war. But in the foreseeable future, according to Leeper's prescription, an elected majority in this highly politicized nation would see the good sense of securing the middle ground from predatory attempts to seize it by the extremes of Left and Right. Given time – Leeper was continually stressing that we were working against the clock – the patient would recover and cure himself of what he analysed to be a dangerous but temporary addiction to the drug of a right-wing monarchist solution. In view of what the poor patient had been through in recent times, addiction to a drug of this nature was understandable. But once on the road to recovery, Leeper was confident that the patient would soon demonstrate a healthy aversion to unnatural and unsuitable therapies. Translated into plain language, this meant as decisive a rejection of the monarchy as of Communism. Macmillan, no less than Leeper, thought the King to be the real 'villain of the piece' in that he was the traditional cause of disunity in the bourgeois parties and, since the winter of 1943, had taken an equivocal stance on the issue of a plebiscite after the war.[23] Leeper believed that a republican centre both should and could be created, and brushed aside the comment that there was a gap – I was amongst those who thought it unbridgeable – between what *could* and what *should* be done in the foreseeable future, when memories were so vivid of December 1944.

[23] Harold Macmillan, *War Diaries 1943-45* (Macmillan, 1984), p. 643.

This was the context in which the choice of Plastiras made sense to both Damaskinos and Leeper as the best available figurehead Prime Minister. Since his coup d'état against King Constantine in 1922, there had been no stain on Plastiras's republican record. Nor was there any sign that he would be soft on Communism. Let that role be reserved for John Sophianopoulos, who was Damaskinos's nominee as Foreign Minister. But at the time it was thought that there might be advantages in having someone like him, known to have left-wing sympathies, to lead the delegation to a meeting in Varkiza, near Athens, with a defeated ELAS.

The resulting agreement on 12 February could not be faulted for its highminded emphasis on an amnesty, the raising of martial law, the purge of the civil service and security services and, most important of all, 'at the earliest possible date and in any case within the current year' a plebiscite and elections, in that order, under international supervision. In view of Britain's role in organizing and even conducting the Varkiza Conference, it was natural for the British Embassy to think that the forces of moderation had won a victory from which the Plastiras government would be the first beneficiary. But Plastiras did not see it that way. First, he was as aware as his Populist rivals that public opinion had already swung decisively over to the right and that the monarchy had benefited – unfairly, of course, in his view. Plastiras's long experience of Greek politics had taught him that the normal way to hold power was to fill the key positions in the Army and the police with his own trusted followers and to instruct them that law and order (which might mean turning a blind eye to right-wing excesses) should take priority over strict observance of the Varkiza agreement. Plastiras's virtues did not include political subtlety and sophistication.

This was not what was expected from a figurehead Prime Minister and it quickly brought Plastiras into conflict, first with Damaskinos, whose nominee as Minister of Interior resigned when he was deprived of the power to enforce the Varkiza agreement, and then with Leeper, who was worried by the likely reaction of public opinion, especially in England, to what could arguably be presented as British sanction in the exchange of one party of violence for another. Leeper even wanted to force

Plastiras to sign an agreement involving the British Embassy's prior approval of his own government's decisions. But fortunately better sense prevailed in the Foreign Office which saw how such a precedent would be welcomed by Stalin in Rumania and Bulgaria, and Churchill needed no convincing. Accordingly, Leeper was instructed that British influence must be exercised behind the scenes and certainly not for all to see in the centre of the stage. Further defections from the Liberal Party led by Gonatas, one of Plastiras's associates in the 1922 coup, showed the growing strength of the royalist cause and further emphasized that Plastiras had lost his grip. When even Sophoulis agreed that the Plastiras experiment had failed, the way was open for Damaskinos, to Leeper's great relief, to appoint a new Prime Minister.

It was therefore to a very different scene that I returned to Athens at the end of March 1945. In April Admiral Voulgaris, as devout an anti-Communist republican as Plastiras (he had suppressed the naval mutiny in Alexandria the year before) was appointed Prime Minister and Minister of Defence in what was called for the first time a 'service' government. Its sole declared purpose was to prepare the country for a plebiscite and elections as soon as possible. It contained such close associates of Damaskinos as Costa Tsatsos who became Minister of the Interior, while Sophianopoulos remained Foreign Minister. His retention, in view of his deserved reputation for wishing to keep in with the Left, infuriated the Populists, led by Panayiotis Tsaldaris and Petros Mavromichalis, who were becoming increasingly hostile to Damaskinos, and disillusioned by Leeper's undisguised conviction that some way must be found to keep the King in London. It was from this time that the Populists made a play on the Regent's ecclesiastical title 'Makariotis' (His Beatitude) and cheerfully nicknamed him 'Maskariotis' (a scoundrel). They made no secret of excusing right-wing terrorism by the National Guard through much of the countryside where, in defiance of the Varkiza agreement, past membership of ELAS was judged to be a crime. The British Embassy was aware of the activities of extremist groups in the Army and the National Guard, and Leeper soon saw the dangers of their growing influence. Indeed, if he had had his way, he would have gone along with Admiral Voulgaris's plan to grant executive powers to the newly formed British Military Mission, including the selection of officers for senior appointments. But once again Leeper was overruled by the Foreign Office, which refused to step into the booby trap of formalizing the powers of the Military Mission. Some disguise, however thin, was needed to counter the charge that Greece was ruled from London.

Meantime, after three months in office, Voulgaris's service government had failed to restore law and order, with its consequent effect on the preparation of the electoral registers. It was also facing serious trouble on the economic front. In early June the courageous policies of Kyriakos Varvaressos, the Minister of Supply, whom Leeper had astutely urged to join the government, were designed to combat the runaway inflation by a series of emergency decrees, levying taxes on industrialists and fixing low prices for the sale of domestically produced commodities and foodstuffs. On this score, opposition to the government stretched from the Populists to the Communist Party. Since the beginning of 1945 Greece had been caught in a vicious circle. A ratified constitution and an elected government were the prerequisites of political stability and the start of economic reconstruction. But no government could be elected until stability had been assured. So once again, Damaskinos and Leeper found themselves facing the prospective failure of their second experiment.

During that summer, after the German surrender in May, and as soon as I was demobilized, Leeper asked me to join the staff of the British Embassy as a Second Secretary. It was therefore in a new capacity, but without a break, that I was able to watch the procession of events over most of the next three years. Some of the leading personalities I had known in Epirus emerged in Athens to become part of new and wider political groupings. Zervas moved steadily to the right; Pyromaglou broke with him and moved no less steadily in the opposite direction. EDES, as I had foreseen a year earlier, did not survive as a party or a movement in the postwar era, which was instantly marked by a vigorous revival of traditional party divisions and the contest between the main prewar political personalities, whom Metaxas had silenced in August 1936. The Communist Party (KKE) also reverted to its prewar leadership under Nikos Zachariades after his release from a German concentration camp in June 1945, and began to prepare for the Third Round of its struggle for power. Soon after my return to Athens I renewed contact with a number of the younger generation of Populists, notably Spiros Theotokis, who had been one of the delegates to the Lebanon Conference in May 1944, Andreas Stratos, and Giorgos Drossos, who was then a leader writer on the royalist newspaper *Ellenikon Aima*. Close contact with these three and their friends made me fully aware of their confidence that public opinion was increasingly on their side in the political debate. I put them in touch with Leeper, so that he could argue with them directly, even if they in no sense changed his views on the feasibility of British objectives. From Kartalis and Yiannis Georgakis, the Regent's *chef de cabinet*, with whom I was also in touch, Leeper heard a different evaluation of the political outlook, which was more in line with his own.

I made no secret of both my surprise and delight when the British Labour Party won the postwar election so convincingly in July 1945. But in the Greek context, I shared the apprehension of many of my colleagues in the Embassy, as we wondered how Attlee and Bevin would handle the unique inheritance of virtually total British responsibility for the internal and external policies of a technically independent country. Sophianopoulos had already pulled out of the government when all Athens was startled by the news of the Labour Party's sweeping victory. It was only with difficulty that Damaskinos persuaded Voulgaris to continue in office, but even he could not prevent the resignations of his own nominees in the two key posts of Minister of the Interior and Minister of Justice. It was then in mid August that Damaskinos took the plunge and opened his campaign to persuade Bevin to switch the order of events in the Varkiza agreement – Leeper had also been toying with the same idea – by postponing the plebiscite until after the elections. In this connection Damaskinos banked on the tactical advantage of Churchill's absence from the scene, as the ultimate protector of King George's interests, and let it be known that he would welcome an early visit to London.

In Leeper's absence, Harold Caccia was given a dress rehearsal by Damaskinos of the performance he would shortly give to Labour ministers in London,[24] to the effect that if the plebiscite

[24] See G. M. Alexander, *The Prelude to the Truman Doctrine* (Clarendon Press, 1982).

took place before the elections it was highly likely that the vote would go in favour of the King, whose return would be only temporarily legitimized, since it would be basically an emotional reaction to the performance of EAM/ELAS in December 1944, and not a reasoned preference for the institution of monarchy. Public opinion would soon swing back against the right-wing government, which the King would inevitably impose. In no time there would be another Left-Right confrontation and Greece would once more be on the verge of catastrophe. On the other hand, if Britain intervened to assist the republican cause by postponing the plebiscite, public opinion would follow Britain's lead and start to shift away from its present preference for the King's return. In this way, the disaster of a political counter-revolution would be avoided. Caccia faithfully relayed Damaskinos's views, but he put this argument in its historical perspective by also pointing out what had happened in Greece between 1922 and 1935, where the facts scarcely validated the equation between a republic and stability.

I was not the only one in the Embassy to accept the theory that the postponement of the plebiscite would reduce support for the King and bring about conditions where the royalists, the republican Right and even the moderate non-Communist Left would see the sense of reconciling their differences. In this way the much-desired centre might emerge, sparing Greece from the seesaw of the two extremes of Left and Right. But the snag, as I and others saw it, was the extreme unlikelihood of the theory being converted into practice. Of course, it would have looked better for a Labour government to have ushered in a republic; but some of us could see no way of making this happen, short of preventing the Greek people from expressing their preferences at the ballot box. Support for the early return of the King, for good or bad reasons and whether or not caused mainly by reaction to the December uprising, was an inescapable fact that could not be changed by political juggling.

Bevin's first statement caused surprise when he announced to the House of Commons on 20 August that it was for the Greeks, not the British, to decide whether or not a plebiscite should precede the elections. Nine days later the Populists came forward with a memorandum to the Regent using the more sophisticated argument that even if the elections preceded the plebiscite, the end result would be the same, for the simple reason that any election would be fought almost exclusively on the constitutional issue. Since early 1945 Leeper had heard this argument put forward a number of times by Tsaldaris and Spiros Theotokis, among others. But he remained consistently unconvinced. The Liberals' response to Populist confidence that the future was theirs in any event was to urge a postponement of the plebiscite for two or three years.

Damaskinos arrived in London on 9 September, shortly after Voulgaris's government had been further weakened by the resignation of Varvaressos. At first the argument was on who should advise whom to delay the plebiscite. Damaskinos wanted to be covered by advice from Britain and the United States. Bevin wanted it the other way round. After much wrangling to and fro, Bevin finally agreed with his American and French counterparts to issue an announcement on 20 September, which called for observers from the three governments – the Soviet Union refused to take part – to be sent to Greece for elections to be held, it was hoped, before the end of the year:

Thus a government would be formed which would be based on the wishes of the people and Parliament . . . Only when these conditions are in due course firmly established, will it become possible to hold a free and genuine plebiscite . . . The three governments hope and recommend that all parties in Greece . . . will collaborate sincerely and willingly in the execution of this programme.

Damaskinos and Leeper flew back to Athens the following day, thinking their dreams had come true. Now there was international recognition of the need to reverse the chronology of events in the Varkiza agreement. But within forty-eight hours they were given a rude shock when, far from 'collaborating sincerely and willingly', the Populists launched their electoral campaign with an appeal to vote for a new parliament which would restore the King to his throne, while the Liberals pressed for the elections to be postponed. As in the game of snakes and ladders, it was 'back to start'.

When the Voulgaris government finally disintegrated in October, there followed the familiar manoeuvres with Leeper wanting a government left of centre and Damaskinos trying once more and failing to bring royalists and republicans into a coalition. For a short and dangerous period, the Regent was his own Prime Minister, while so genuine were the fears of a royalist coup d'état in Athens that Bevin had to send Damaskinos a personal message assuring him that British troops would put down any such rebellion. On 2 November Panayiotis Kanellopoulos put together a government, which lasted a matter of weeks. At the end of November Damaskinos, after seriously threatening to resign himself (at this point U.S. Ambassador MacVeagh played a key role in holding him up to his responsibilities), was persuaded to install Sophoulis, who was over eighty, as Prime Minister. A government was formed which included leading members of the traditional Liberal centre and Sophianopoulos returned to the Foreign Ministry. With the exception of the latter, these were the kind of people whom Leeper had long wanted to see in office. But what gave him most satisfaction was his success in persuading Sophoulis to accept the appointments of some of the leading members of the non-Communist wartime Resistance, notably Kartalis and Georgakis, who had been the Regent's *chef de cabinet*. Leeper had first met Kartalis when he represented EKKA in the *andarte* delegation that visited Cairo in the summer of 1943. At that time he had formed a distinctly low opinion of him. The opposite was the case when they met after the war. In fact, throughout 1945 Kartalis had played an important role in influencing Leeper's political evaluations.

No sooner had Sophoulis's cabinet been formed than the familiar in-fighting began between the Kaphandaris and Tsouderos factions over the date of the elections, which Sophoulis announced for 31 March 1946 on the proportional representation system which favoured small parties like his own. This decision angered the Populists, who were aware that it would reduce the size of their electoral victory, and also a section of the Liberal Party, led by Sophocles Venizelos, who wanted a later date to give more time for organizing the party's political machinery. Other divisive issues within the Cabinet were the management of the amnesty and the size of the British loan to restore confidence in the value of the drachma and counter the price of the gold sovereign, which was rocketing higher every week. The KKE, which had originally given Sophoulis the benefit of the doubt, was soon accusing his government of condoning the reign of right-wing terror, and on 12 December *Rizospastis* gave the first indication that Communists would abstain from what it called Sophoulis's electoral farce.

The domestic situation was internationalized on 21 January 1946 – the day after right-wing extremists of the 'X' organization had taken temporary control of Kalamata in the Peloponnese – when the Soviet Union lodged a formal protest with the United Nations Security Council against the presence of British troops in Greece. Sophoulis stood firm and sacked Sophianopoulos when the latter disobeyed his instructions to rebut the Soviet case. This incident was a turning point in that the KKE isolated itself in its lone support of the Soviet diplomatic offensive. At the same time, the context of Sophianopoulos's dismissal emphasized what had been true for at least the whole of the previous year: that Greece had to choose between the polarized options of a Communist Left and monarchist Right. British policy had been expressly designed to avoid this situation; but the third alternative remained as elusive as ever.

On 1 February 1946 Bevin delivered an extremely firm speech to the Security Council, rightly insisting that British troops were in Greece for the sole purpose of securing conditions for free elections, after which they would be withdrawn. He was therefore all the more irritated, to put it mildly, when Leeper backed Sophoulis's proposed trade-off to broaden his government if elections could be postponed for two months. On 8 February Leeper received strict instructions to press Sophoulis not to flinch from the agreed date of 31 March and ten days later Sophoulis acquiesced. His decision cost him the departure of Merkouris, the Minister of Public Order, with whom I had kept in touch since our first meeting in December 1944 at the height of the Battle of Athens. Sir Charles Wickham, the head of the Police Mission, had been complaining to Leeper about Merkouris's political appointments in the gendarmerie, while Merkouris had barked back that Greece was not the same as Wickham's native Ulster. To me, Merkouris had been reiterating the same theme for months: that no fair elections could be held until right-wing terrorism had been suppressed. This meant a postponement from 31 March until much later in 1946, perhaps even until November if, in his view, there was to be any hope of preventing a Populist victory. Merkouris's resignation was followed in early March by declarations from Kaphandaris and Kartalis, who both announced that they would abstain from the elections. This caused no surprise, since the 'Eleftheria group', as we called it in the British Embassy (the name came from the newspaper of which Kartalis was a member of the editorial board), had been advocating that the elections should be postponed for eight months since early February. Equally unsurprising at the time was Zachariades's ruling in February at the 2nd Plenum of the KKE's Central Committee in favour of abstention, which was to cause such subsequent controversy within the Communist Party. This lead was followed in March by a similar stand from Sophianopoulos and the moderate left grouping, headed by Svolos and Tsirimokos, who had distanced themselves from the Communist position in the early days of Sophoulis's government. Hence the third experiment was in sight of failure.

Leeper's transfer, three weeks before the elections, spared him the painful experience of witnessing the victory of the Populist Party, which won 208 of the 238 royalist seats (most of the remainder went to Zervas's recently formed National Party), out of a total of 354. The temporary republican electoral grouping of Papandreou, Venizelos and Kanellopoulos came second with 67 seats, and Sophoulis's Liberal party a poor third with 48 seats, in spite of being in political control in the vital run up to the election. The Allied Mission for Observing the Greek Elections (AMFOGE) concluded that 'notwithstanding the present intensity of political emotions in Greece, conditions were such as to warrant the holding of elections . . . and the general outcome represented a true and valid verdict of the Greek people'.

The introduction of Sir Clifford Norton to the political scene marked no sharp break from the Leeper regime. He began by going through the normal motions of a British Ambassador trying to influence events by urging Tsaldaris, flushed with the victory of the Populist Party, to broaden his government by including Papandreou, Venizelos and Kanellopoulos, and also to postpone the plebiscite. At first this looked like succeeding when all three took office as Ministers without portfolio. But within a fortnight they had resigned after all the important posts had been filled by Populists, and after Tsaldaris, who had come under pressure from newly elected members of his party, refused to budge on the issue of an early plebiscite. Fortunately for Tsaldaris, Bevin quickly changed his mind, seeing the advantage of conducting the plebiscite while British troops were still in Greece. He hoped that their presence would act as a restraint on the right and prevent a runaway victory for the King. By the same token, there were foreseeable international repercussions if British troops were to remain for another two years. An additional factor favouring an early plebiscite was American agreement that the job should be finished quickly. So when Norton informed Tsaldaris that Bevin had agreed to a plebiscite in the autumn, the scene was set for Damaskinos to preside over the first session of parliament on 13 May and proclaim that the plebiscite would be held on 1 September.

As each week passed, the British government became increasingly sensitive to the charge that it was the prop behind an illiberal administration, which set up courts martial to deal with left-wing terrorism in northern Greece, but which neglected to take similar action against what the British Police Mission estimated to be about the same number of right-wing offences in the Peloponnese. In order to press his case in person, Tsaldaris left Athens at the end of June, saw Bevin briefly in Paris and had a number of meetings in early July with Clement Attlee and Hugh Dalton, and also with Averell Harriman, then American Ambassador in London. The visit was a personal failure in that he returned to Athens without the Anglo-American support on which he had counted, both for additional economic aid for reconstruction and for Greece's territorial claims against Albania and Bulgaria. It was also a rebuff to Tsaldaris's pride that the Foreign Office put increased pressure on him to show that justice was being impartially administered in the prelude to the plebiscite. While Tsaldaris's government could rely on wide support in July for its disregard of the KKE's call in *Rizospastis* for reconciliation, it was quite another matter when the Populist Party had to drum up support for as vigorous an anti-Communist as Spiros Theotokis, then Minister of Public Order, against a parliamentary motion of censure brought against him by Zervas for failing to stamp out Communist activity. As head of the

National Party, Zervas had become the leader of the intransigent Right, with which no one in the British Embassy had any sympathy. At the same time, Mavromichalis, the Minister of Defence, was known to have a hand in the activities of royalist terrorists in the Peloponnese. Sadly, all the British Embassy could do was to make a forlorn request on the eve of the plebiscite for restraint on 1 September.

When the vote was counted, the government claimed an overall majority of 68 per cent in favour of the King. In the Peloponnese, the royalist vote took over 90 per cent; but in Macedonia it was only 67 per cent and in Piraeus, Salonika and Crete there were majority votes against the King's return. The AMFOGE observers reported that conditions were plainly unsuitable in certain areas for a fair plebiscite, but even so their considered verdict was that a majority vote had gone in favour of the King.

On 28 September 1946 King George arrived in Athens for his second restoration, and was greeted by a delirious demonstration of spontaneous enthusiasm. His temporary transformation into a popular hero was attributable to the events of December 1944 and their consequences rather than to any action taken by himself or his followers. He was in a sober mood, resentful that successive British governments had kept him waiting so long. He was conscious of the need to broaden Tsaldaris's government and needed no briefing on the fact that the Third Round of the Civil War was already under way. The fighting, which had broken out in northern Greece shortly after Tsaldaris had formed his first Populist government, had gathered momentum during the summer. Indeed, a sharp increase in Communist guerrilla activity had been noticed soon after the plebiscite.

Within a week of the King's return, Norton was following the usual Foreign Office instruction to press the King not to give up trying, after his first failure, to persuade Sophoulis to join a new Cabinet. But the new factor was the action of American Ambassador MacVeagh, who on 11 October took even stronger action and urged the King to put his foot down and insist on a broadened coalition. Shortly before, the Foreign Office had been informed by the American Embassy in London that a detailed programme of assistance for Greece had been agreed in Washington. On 15 October Secretary of State Byrnes informed the British

Minister of Defence during their meeting in Paris that America was now ready to take the lead in strengthening Greece and Turkey. These were among the first moves in a new American initiative. Thereafter Norton and MacVeagh were riding in double harness, but soon MacVeagh would be in front.

During the early autumn of 1946, the Third Round of the Civil War had spread from northern Greece to the Peloponnese; and in October Markos Vaphiades announced the creation of a Communist 'Democratic Army'. The plebiscite had also coincided with a sharp deterioration in Greek-Yugoslav relations, which resulted in Tsaldaris appearing before the U. N. Security Council in December and accusing Yugoslavia, Albania and Bulgaria of fomenting rebellion in northern Greece with the aim of annexing 'Aegean Macedonia'. But his visits to London and Washington before and after the debate in the Security Council did nothing to change the low opinion of his competence and suitability as Prime Minister, which was shared by the British and American governments. Both would have liked to see Greece governed from a broader political base, in order to project a more moderate image to public opinion, especially abroad. Such a prospect was no less welcome to King George.

From October onwards, there had been, with good reason, a steadily growing concern in Washington with Greek affairs. By the end of 1946 the situation had greatly deteriorated and a fully fledged civil war was under way, in spite of the huge British commitment in the form of military, naval and air force missions, in addition to economic, financial, legal and police missions. Yet the paradox remained that despite this embarrassingly evident British presence, the Embassy was not in control of Greek affairs.

A prolonged series of moves by the British and American Ambassadors, Norton and MacVeagh, to reshape the government ultimately resulted in Tsaldaris's welcome resignation and his replacement in January 1947 by Dimitrios Maximos, a former Governor of the National Bank, who at the age of seventy-three was widely accepted as a neutral figure. This allowed Papandreou, Venizelos and Kanellopoulos to take important posts in the government, and soon after Zervas became Minister of Public Order – in spite of an attempt by the British Embassy to block his appointment.

A better-looking government did not, however, alter the fact that Greece was on the verge of economic collapse, in spite of an infusion of £39 million in British aid since the end of the war. Greece still desperately needed political and military support if the country was to preserve its independence. In February 1947, the British Cabinet decided that it could no longer continue to carry the burden of its former responsibilities and instructed the British Ambassador in Washington to inform the State Department of the extremely urgent need of American intervention. On 12 March 1947 President Truman requested $400 million of emergency aid from Congress and announced that the policy of the United States would henceforth be directed toward the active assistance of free peoples, who were resisting attempted subjugation by armed minorities or outside pressure. From that moment onward, the British government played a secondary role in Greek affairs.

In April 1947 King Paul succeeded to the throne after his elder brother's sudden death. The new King began with the initial advantage of not having been personally involved in the enmities his predecessor had fostered with such a broad and varied segment of the Greek political world. But his succession coincided with the accelerated pace of an undisguised civil war. In June 1947 Markos Vaphiades's Democratic Army made a bold attempt to seize Konitsa, near the Albanian border, and hold it as the rebels' provisional capital. In September a Liberal-Populist coalition was formed under Sophoulis: it offered an amnesty to the rebels, which fell on deaf ears. In the meantime, the American Mission for Aid to Greece (AMAG) was supplying weaponry, equipment and operational advice which more than counterbalanced what Vaphiades was receiving from Greece's northern neighbours. In November 1947 a Joint General Staff was created by the Greek and American governments to fight the expanding civil war. On Christmas Eve 1947 Vaphiades proclaimed a 'free government' in northern Greece. This led to the Communist Party being officially outlawed by the Athens authorities as the final political development of that year.

For me 1946 and 1947 had been two highly charged and – in a personal way – exceptionally happy years, when I had submerged myself with undiluted pleasure in the Greek way of life. This meant sharing with my Greek friends their fascination with political controversy, which so often revolved round allegiance to individuals rather than to political programmes. But it also meant participating in their liberal allowances of time to relax, laugh, gossip, eat, drink, dance, make merry and in general treat enjoyment as the first priority in life. Wars, foreign occupations, civil wars, profound political uncertainty about the future were only part of life. They were not everything if you had eyes and ears and a healthy human appetite for all the other compensations that life had to offer. A discussion with a friend like Manos Gregoriou, a close follower of Sophoulis, was as likely to take place over lunch or dinner in a taverna as in an office. The same applied to my privileged meetings with members of the active Athens press, notably George Vlachos, the founder and editor of the Populist newspaper *Kathemerini*, and his talented daughter, Eleni, who was to inherit her father's position, or with their political rival Dimitrios Lambrakis, the editor of *Vima*.

Mercifully, politics was not my only preoccupation. Much of my spare time outside the Embassy was spent with Steven Runciman visiting Byzantine churches and learning from him what to look for when buying icons, tanagras, Mycenean and Black Attic pottery, all of which were at that time purchasable from my modest salary. He, Rex Warner and Paddy Leigh Fermor were organizing the rebirth of the British Council in Greece and bringing it unprecedented renown. Through them I was introduced to the literary world, two of whose leading figures became my friends: George Sepheriades, the diplomat whose poetry published under the name Sepheris was later to win him a Nobel Prize, and George Katsimbalis, known to Anglo-Saxon readers from Henry Miller's *Colossos of Maroussi*, who brought me an understanding of the poetry of Palamas, Cavafy and Sikelianos and the novels of Kazantzakis, Prevelakis, Venezis and Myrivilis. A memorable event in this connection during the summer of 1946 was when Maurice Bowra made his triumphant return after the war from Oxford to Athens. Rex Warner, Paddy Leigh Fermor and I organized a marathon lunch party for him at a taverna by the sea to meet Sepheriades and Katsimbalis. As soon as we had sat down, we all started eating, drinking and talking like gunfire. The lunch ended six hours later. There was also the theatre, which filled many an evening and brought me in touch with the well-known actor Takis Horn, the director Alexis Solomos and others in their profession.

Early in the new year 1948, I was warned that my time in Athens was drawing to a close. In April I was posted to Jerusalem and arrived just in time to watch the start of the first Arab-Israeli War. I therefore left Greece more than a year before the national Army, greatly helped by the Air Force, fought and won its battles in the Grammos and Vitsi Mountains, thereby forcing the remnants of Markos Vaphiades's guerrillas to escape across the border into Albania in the late summer of 1949.

I had arrived in Greece soon after the start of the First Round in late 1943. In November 1949, soon after the end of the Third Round, I flew back for a happy return to Athens in order to marry Maria Tambacopoulou in a small church beneath the Acropolis. Thereafter, Greece and Greeks became permanent fixtures in the normal course of a wandering life between the Foreign Office and its posts abroad.

I did not, however, go back to Tseritsana until 1973. By then it was a short drive to the village along a manageable road from Ioannina. When I had last done this journey in reverse in 1944, it had been a seven-hour walk over mountain footpaths. On the way to Tseritsana, even much of the lie of the land seemed new to me and it was not until the car began to climb the hill leading into the village that I was sure I had come to the right place. Then, suddenly, everything was familiar. I saw the fountain under the tall plane trees, where the village was gathered for the morning gossip. In this scene, no detail had changed. As I drove towards them I wondered if I would find a single person whose memory stretched back to the time I had lived there.

My wife walked up to the fountain and asked if there was anyone who might by chance have heard of a Captain Jim during the war. To her surprise and even more to mine, one of them recognized the name and announced in a shrill voice: 'Jim is back!' Then they clustered around the car asking where we had come from, whom we intended to see and how long we were going to stay: questions that would have been put at any time to any new arrival in the village. There was the same warmth and spontaneous curiosity that I remembeed so vividly from a distant past.

Lunch was prepared and a stream of reminiscences soon began to flow from our host, who was one of the very few to have remained in the village since the war. The cross-questioning came from both sides. I produced a string of names to learn that most of the people were either dead or had not been heard of for years. Two things, however, emerged in our conversation that showed the contrast between my wartime experience and the later transformation of their lives, especially over the previous ten years.

The first was their detailed recollection, not blurred by time, of December 1944 when ELAS occupied the village. As full-scale civil war spread from Athens to the rest of Greece, Zervas was defeated and forced to abandon Epirus and take refuge in Corfu at the turn of the year with some 6,000 members of EDES and 7-8,000 refugees. This brought ELAS into occupation of the whole of Lakka Souli; special vengeance was taken on the villages where support for Zervas had been strongest. Tseritsana was one of them. The horror and miseries of that brief period, we were told, made the burning and sacking of the village at the end of 1943 by the Germans pale into insignificance. I had heard this last story many times while I lived there. It was one of the reasons I had chosen Tseritsana as a base in the first place, because the Germans rarely took the trouble to burn a village twice.

The villagers' references to a different Germany showed how the wheel had come full circle. As we walked over the village after lunch, I was struck by the fact that there were no young men to be seen. Before I asked the reason, the answer was given that the only people left to work on the land were those who were too old to have emigrated. A whole generation had left to become happily and prosperously installed in Germany since the early sixties. From there the benefits of an economic boom had flowed back in regular remittances to their families. It seemed a strangely civilized culmination of the story.

One tiny incident on the drive back brought the day to an end. Some way ahead of us, I noticed a solitary black figure, who turned out to be a village priest, striding down the road. As we drove past him, we naturally stopped to offer him a lift. The normal interrogation then began. What wind, he asked, had brought us there? Where had we been and whom had we seen? I explained how and why Tseritsana had once been my home. At this there was a shout of surprise and he seemed astonished that I did not remember him, Nikos, since he, too, had been an *andarte* with Zervas. In a gesture that was symbolic but unconscious, he threw off his priest's black hat and became an *andarte* again, recalling where and how he had fought against the Germans, and how many of them he had killed in each engagement. He had been born in mountain Epirus and was proud never to have left it. For him there was nothing odd in the continuity of his life when the war ended and he became a priest. We dropped him a few miles further on, as he was making for two isolated villages, which we could see from the road, where a marriage and a christening awaited his arrival. Nikos, the priest, was the last link with this slice of my life.

Index